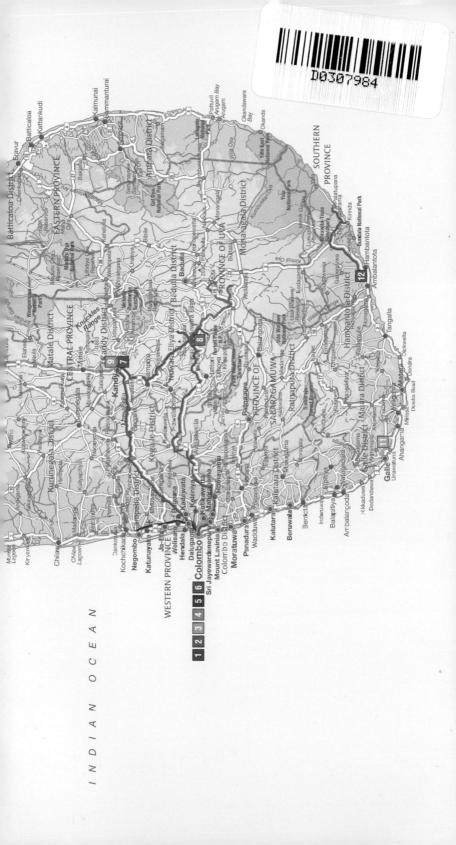

INSIGHT GUIDES

SRI LANKA

Step by Step

APA PUBLICATIONS
Part of the Langenscheidt Publishing Group

CONTENTS

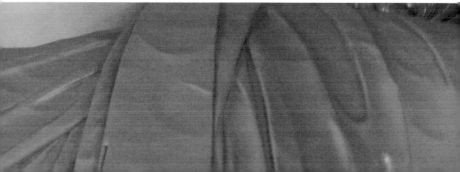

ABOUT THIS BOOK

This *Step by Step Guide* has been produced by the editors of Insight Guides, whose books have set the standard for visual travel guides since 1970. With top-quality photography and authoritative recommendations, this guidebook brings you the very best of Sri Lanka in a series of 12 tailor-made tours.

WALKS AND TOURS

The tours in the book provide something to suit all budgets, tastes and trip lengths. They begin with two tours of Sri Lanka's capital, Colombo, followed by a series of drives and walks that move through Colombo's environs, the country's hilly interior, the Cultural Triangle and finish on the south coast. The tours embrace a range of interests, so whether you are an architecture fan, a keen shopper, a lover of flora or want to chill out on the beach, you will find an option to suit.

We recommend that you read the whole of a tour before setting out. This should help you to familiarise yourself with the route and enable you to plan where to stop for refreshments

– options for this are shown in the 'Food and Drink' boxes, recognisable by the knife-and-fork sign, on most pages.

For our pick of the walks by theme, consult Recommended Tours For… *(see pp.6–7)*.

OVERVIEW

The tours are set in context by this introductory section, giving an overview of the city to set the scene, plus background information on food and drink, shopping, entertainment and sports. A succinct history timeline highlights the key events that have shaped Sri Lanka over the centuries.

DIRECTORY

Also supporting the tours is a Directory chapter, comprising a user-friendly, clearly organised A–Z of practical information, our pick of where to stay while you are in the city and select restaurant listings; these eateries complement the more low-key cafés and restaurants that feature within the tours and are intended to offer a wider choice for evening dining.

Above: hill country swathed in cloud; Buddha at the Seema Malakaya, Colombo; Negombo Beach; Pinnawela Elephant Orphanage; Presidential Secretariat, Colombo, with modern buildings behind.

The Author

Royston Ellis retired from being a rock 'n' roll poet when he was 20 and left England for a life of travel that took him around the world several times. He lived in Dominica for 16 years before settling in Sri Lanka in 1980, where he lives near Bentota in a colonial cottage overlooking the Indian Ocean. Since his first paperback book, *The Big Beat Scene*, was published in 1961, he has written 60 novels, biographies and travel guides, and hundreds of articles for international newspapers and in-flight magazines about his favourite country, Sri Lanka. Some of the tours in this book were originally conceived by Vijitha Yapa.

Margin Tips
Shopping tips, historical facts, handy hints and information on activities help visitors to make the most of their time in Sri Lanka.

Feature Boxes
Notable topics are highlighted in these special boxes.

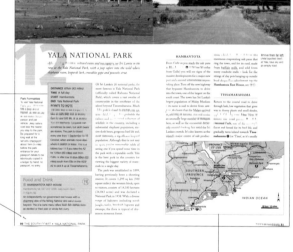

Key Facts Box
This box gives details of the distance covered on the tour, plus an estimate of how long it should take. It also states where the route starts and finishes, and gives key travel information such as which days are best to do the route or handy transport tips.

Footers
Look here for the tour name, a map reference and the main attraction on the double-page.

Food and Drink
Recommendations of where to stop for refreshment are given in these boxes. The numbers prior to each restaurant/café name link to references in the main text. Restaurants in the Food and Drink boxes are plotted on the maps.

The $ signs at the end of each entry reflect the approximate cost of a two-course meal for one. These should be seen as a guide only. Price ranges, also quoted on the inside back flap for easy reference, are:

$$$$	over Rs2,500
$$$	Rs1,250–2,500
$$	Rs500–1,250
$	below Rs500

Route Map
Detailed cartography shows the tour clearly plotted with numbered dots. For more detailed mapping, see the pull-out map slotted inside the back cover.

ANCIENT TEMPLES

Marvel at cave temples and ruins of ancient shrines (tour 9), pay homage at the medieval Temple of the Tooth (tour 6) or visit artistically restored temples in Colombo (tour 2).

RECOMMENDED TOURS FOR...

ANIMAL-LOVERS

Animals are one of Sri Lanka's many attractions: you can see adorable orphaned elephants (tour 6), go on jungle safaris (tours 10 and 12) or get up close to creatures in the park-like zoo near Colombo (tour 4).

BEACHES

Laze on Negombo's sandy stretch (tour 5), promenade on Mount Lavinia's golden strand (tour 4) or head to Unawatuna, Sri Lanka's most popular resort with a charming cove and a laidback atmosphere (tour 11).

BOTANICAL GARDENS

Get back to nature at Sri Lanka's three very different botanical gardens (tours 6 and 7) and dry-zone arboretum, where you can meander along the trails under ghostly tropical trees (tour 9).

COLONIAL ARCHITECTURE

You can discover ornate British colonial buildings in Colombo Fort and inspiring Dutch designs in Pettah (walk 1), or a time-warp amalgamation of both in Galle Fort (tour 11).

HOTTEST CURRIES

If hotel food is too bland, search for spicier cuisine in Kandy (tour 6), in rest houses (tours 7 and 8) or in speciality restaurants in Colombo serving Sri Lankan food (tour 2).

MOUNTAIN VIEWS

Hike to World's End for fabulous mountain-top views down to the south coast, or get a glimpse of Mount Pidurutalagala, Sri Lanka's highest peak, from Nuwara Eliya (tour 7); or scramble up to Lipton's Seat (tour 8) for breath-taking vistas through the clouds.

RAIL BUFFS

Get up early one morning to make the pleasantly rickety rail journey to Homagama (tour 3), or from Colombo or Kandy venture on a train trip to Nanu Oya and the hill country (tour 7).

SHOPPERS

Colombo is home to air-conditioned shopping malls and trendy boutiques selling unusual souvenirs (tour 2), and there are quaint shops and art galleries in Galle Fort (tour 11).

TEA TREKKING

Trek through tea gardens to your heart's content at Kandapola (tour 7) and Haputale (tour 8), relishing the cool mountain air, then warm up with a cup of pure Ceylon tea in a plantation bungalow.

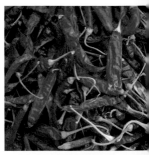

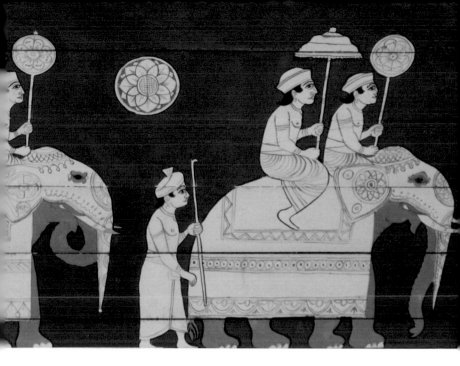

OVERVIEW

An overview of Sri Lanka's geography, customs and culture, plus illuminating background information on food and drink, shopping, entertainment, sports and relaxation, and history.

INTRODUCTION

With its endless miles of golden beaches and abundant natural riches, for many visitors Sri Lanka is one of Asia's ultimate tropical island paradises – but it also has tremendous physical, cultural and ethnic diversity, as well as a long and distinguished history enriched by centuries of foreign influence.

Above: Buddha at the Gangaramaya Temple in Colombo; the lotus flower is sacred to Buddhists.

Sun and Heat
Sunburn and even sunstroke are a risk in lowland Sri Lanka, whether you're lying on the beach or exploring ancient monuments. An umbrella is never out of place; you may need it to keep the rain off, or for shelter from the sun.

The shape of Sri Lanka has evoked visions of a teardrop falling from the tip of India, but a mango is a more appropriate likeness. True, the past has given rise to tears, but the island is so abundantly blessed by nature's bounty, it is – like a mango – a treat to savour.

During 26 years of civil war, the country was spurned by most tourists. Today, Sri Lanka remains little changed since the war began, making it a haven for the individual seeking a holiday in a traditional social and ecological environment.

GEOGRAPHY AND LAYOUT

Sri Lanka is a small country with a land area of 65,525 sq km (25,299 sq miles); it is 435km (271 miles) from top to bottom, and 240km (149 miles) from east to west. Lying a few degrees north of the Equator in the balmy waters of the Indian Ocean, the island has an incredibly diverse range of landscapes, from sultry tropical beaches, coconut plantations and lowland jungles of the coast to the cool green hill country with its mist-shrouded mountains, crashing waterfalls and endless tea plantations.

Exploring the Country
The island's size and newly rebuilt main highways make it easy to travel between its best sights within the space of a few days. The tours outlined in this book have been designed to help the reader gain an insight into Sri Lanka's beauty while becoming acquainted with its enchanting people.

The starting point for most visitors is the commercial capital, Colombo *(tours 1 and 2)*, and this can be explored easily on foot or by the ubiquitous three-wheeler taxis (tuk-tuks). From Colombo, you can make excursions to its surrounding attractions *(tours 3–5)* or an overnight trip to Sri Lanka's cultural capital, Kandy *(tour 6)*. With a few more days spare, you can drive north from Kandy to the ancient capitals *(tours 9 and 10)* or discover the charms of the hill country *(tours 7 and 8)* and then journey to the Yala National Park *(tour 12)* in the south before returning to Colombo via Galle Fort *(tour 11)*.

Every tour yields something astonishing, from orphan elephants bathing to the evocative ruins of ancient capitals, the natural beauty of the hill country and the allure of boutique hotels.

HISTORY AND ARCHITECTURE

The first humans to arrive were the aboriginal Veddhas, who walked across from India 16,000 years ago. Around the 4th century BC, immigrants from North India began to arrive, becoming ancestors of the modern Sinhalese.

Early development of the island was mainly in the northern half, where the ancient ruins of Anuradhapura and Polonnaruwa testify to a glorious Buddhist culture and pioneering land development, including inland waterways and reservoirs (tanks) to foster agriculture.

After the 13th century, the island was fragmented, and in 1597 Kandy became the seat of a hill kingdom allied with smaller kingdoms in the south. The 16th century also saw the arrival of the Portuguese, beginning the interest of European powers in the island.

In 1656 the Dutch arrived and built grand mansions, adapting their building and furnishing styles to tropical conditions. With rooms built around central open-air courtyards and doors in line with each other, air could flow through unimpeded to keep houses cool.

The British weighed in from the start of the 19th century, with heavy Victorian and Edwardian buildings linked by broad boulevards that became the wide main roads of the cities.

Modern Sri Lankan architecture has been dominated by the work of architect Geoffrey Bawa (1919–2003),

Above from far left: hilly Dambulla landscape; a golden stretch near Bentota; a guardstone at the entrance to Polonnaruwa's ancient Vatadage.

Left: Kandy's lakeside Temple of the Tooth and Royal Bathhouse.

Giving Gifts

If you are lucky enough to be invited to a local home, a present of a box of biscuits or even something you've brought with you from overseas, like a souvenir ornament or duty-free chocolate, would be appreciated.

whose concern with nature and the natural setting of his buildings, and the forms of Dutch colonial villas and traditional Sinhalese *walauwe* (houses), created a style which continues to shape the work of many younger designers.

Civil War

The turmoil of centuries of wars against invaders was reflected in the recent past, when the struggle spearheaded by the Liberation Tigers of Tamil Eelam (LTTE) against the government plunged Sri Lanka into a deadly 26-year civil war that only ended in 2009.

Many lives were also lost in 2004, when Sri Lanka was hit by the catastrophic Asian tsunami. Now, having overcome political and natural disasters, an important new stage in the island's turbulent history has been reached.

CLIMATE

The island's climate is so diverse that in one day it is possible to travel from tropical heat to cool mists and even on to the dry zone. There are two separate monsoon seasons, one in the northeast, the other in the southwest – from October to April, the climate is kindest in the southwest, while there is less rain in the northeast from May to October. Expect high humidity and temperatures on the coast of around 27°C (81°F). Kandy, at 305m (1,000ft), averages 20°C (68°F), and Nuwara Eliya, at 1,890m (6,200ft), 16°C (61°F).

POPULATION

While Sri Lanka's racial diversity has caused much strife, it compensates with a diversity of culture and mutual respect between the different races despite the long-raging civil war. Interracial rivalry is fought out with games of 'we got here first', with both the Sinhalese and the Tamils arguing about precedence.

The island's population is overwhelmingly Sinhalese Buddhist. The Sinhalese migrated to Sri Lanka from North India around the 4th century BC. The Tamils are Sri Lanka's second-largest ethnic group, comprising around 18 percent of the population. They claim that their Dravidian ancestors got to the island even earlier. Some 5 percent of the Tamil population are descendants of immigrants brought by the British for plantation labour. Most Sri Lankan Tamils are Hindus.

Sri Lanka's Muslims can trace their presence back for over a millennium, having arrived as merchants, and now mostly live on the east coast. One of the island's smallest but most colourful ethnic groups is the Burghers – white, English-speaking Sri Lankans descended from European settlers, mainly Dutch and Portuguese.

The population is mainly rural (about 80 percent, including those on estate settlements). Since vast tracks of mountainous jungle and arid plains are uninhabited, the population density is high, resulting in crowded townships.

LOCAL CUSTOMS

Sri Lankans are a very friendly and helpful people, and will often ask you where you are from. However, beware of touts who make a living out of preying on tourists. Do not be surprised if a villager invites you home for tea or a meal. In the evening it is the custom for Sri Lankans to have a drink together before eating quite late; people generally go home immediately after the meal rather than stay on for more drinks.

People are not camera shy, but if you want to take a photo, always ask first. Sometimes they will request a copy.

Sri Lankans will forgive many breaches of etiquette, such as your eating habits *(see p.88)*. However, when entering temples, remove your shoes and headgear as a sign of respect. Remember to be sensitive to local religious and cultural customs.

POLITICS AND ECONOMICS

Sri Lanka is a parliamentary democracy with an elected executive president. The 225 members of parliament are elected separately through a complicated proportional voting system. There are scores of registered political parties, all somewhat left-wing and keen on government involvement in more than state affairs, although the tea plantations are no longer nationalised.

Economics
The top foreign-exchange earners are the manufacture of garments exported to the West and inward remittances from Sri Lankans working overseas. Tourism comes third. Agriculture (especially tea exporting) has lost its relative importance to the Sri Lankan economy. It employs 31 percent of the working population, but accounts for only about 12 percent of GDP.

The service sector is the largest component of GDP at around 60 percent. Industry accounts for 28 percent of GDP, with manufacturing of food, beverages and tobacco being the largest subsector.

The per capita income of the 20 million inhabitants is more than US$700. The people of Sri Lanka enjoy free education and healthcare, and a literacy rate of 92 percent – one of the highest in Asia. Now peace has come, the nation hopes it is time for its full potential to be realised.

Above from far left: keeping cool in school uniform in Colombo; a dip at sunset in Negombo; poster of President Mahinda Rajapakse.

Winds of Fortune

The trade winds, on which the monsoons are carried to Sri Lanka, not only keep the island watered, but also helped make it rich. In former centuries the winds provided a reliable shuttle service for traders from Greece, China, Arabia and Rome, sailing in search of spices and gems. Since these seafaring merchants had to wait for the winds to change direction before they could sail home, many decided to stay and set up business instead, developing the island's trade.

FOOD AND DRINK

Sri Lankan cuisine may not be renowned beyond the island's shores, but it is a distinctive and delicious blend of flavours based on local ingredients and spices, and not necessarily stacked with chillies.

Above: Sri Lankan chefs are liberal with the chillies; bananas for sale in Kandy.

Vegetarian Curries
Rice and curry meals, served at the table in bowls or on buffets, always have the meat or fish curries cooked and served separately from the vegetable curries, so vegetarians can select what to eat without qualms.

Over centuries, Sri Lanka's visitors and invaders have contributed Indian, Chinese, Malay and Arab influences, as well as Portuguese, Dutch and British dishes. In hotel buffets you might encounter all of them at the same time, so take the chance to sample what Sri Lanka can offer. Do not be put off by the bland set meals served for Western tourists, as real Sri Lankan food is much more exciting.

LOCAL CUISINE

Sri Lankan curries have a reputation for being deliciously hot, thanks to the generous addition of chillies by enthusiastic cooks. The cooks need to be enthusiastic because of the hours of preparation involved in cooking a good curry. Sri Lankan cooks don't reach for a packet of curry powder; they spend hours grinding selected spices to create a dish that is rich in flavour as well as pungent.

The method of preparation has evolved over the centuries, with a dash of influence by Portuguese settlers in the 16th century. The abundance of fresh vegetables (some introduced by the British in the 19th century) and

forest roots, as well as locally grown spices like cardamom, cinnamon, cloves and the unique ingredient called curry leaves – known as *karapincha* in Sinhala – contribute to making Sri Lankan curries special. This small green leaf adds a distinctive flavour; when crushed it has an aroma akin to lime and sesame. It has the reputation of being good for lowering cholesterol.

The hottest curries are to be found in Galle, Jaffna and Colombo. Meat or fish, and vegetables like eggplant, cabbage, beans and even pineapple, lend themselves to hot curries. Root vegetables and cashew nuts work better as mild curries. Curries cooked in the traditional way – in a clay pot over a wood fire – take on more spicy flavour, thanks to the time taken to cook them.

Rice is the staple, and there are over 15 varieties in Sri Lanka. A favourite is the red country rice, *kakuluhaal*. This strain is full of vitamins and has a nutty flavour, as the grains are left unpolished. White rice, whether the ball-shaped *sambha*, the long-grained *basmati* or the white *milchard*, is widely available.

While Sri Lankans have been raised to expect their curries to be hot in strength, visitors are served milder ver-

sions, tamed by the addition of coconut milk. The curries will be flavoured with different spices to match the main ingredient, whether it's prawns or peas.

BREAKFAST

Appa (hoppers), a type of pancake with crispy edges and made of rice flour or plain flour with coconut milk and yeast, is a favourite Sri Lankan breakfast dish. It can also be served with a fried egg nestling in it and is sensational when eaten with a beef curry and *seeni sambol*, a sweet, spicy onion relish.

Kiribath (milk rice) is a breakfast dish made with rice, cooked in coconut cream or fresh milk and spices. This is considered an auspi-

cious meal and is eaten during special occasions – on the first of each month, or when welcoming visitors.

LUNCH

Lunch packets of rice and curry (usually rice with three vegetable curries and one meat curry) are the mainstay of office workers. Packets are available in simple cafés throughout Colombo. When Sri Lankans are touring the country, they lunch in rest houses or somewhere like the Tea Castle at Talawakele *(see tour 7)*. There a typical spread would consist of curries made of plantain blossoms, radishes, lentils, beef, fish, beans and eggplant, accompanied by bitter *gourd sambol* (a relish), *gotakola medun* (a leaf

salad), devilled potatoes, a spicy mango chutney, and papadum served with fried red chillies and chunks of dry fish.

DINNER

For dinner at home, a Sri Lankan might have a curry served with *indiappa* (string hoppers), a Sri Lankan invention that resembles fine noodles. It is made by squeezing a mixture of rice flour (or plain flour) and water through a colander onto bamboo trays and then steam-cooking the mix until it's fluffy.

String-hopper *biriyani* – a lunch or dinner delicacy – is produced by breaking *indiappa* into small pieces and then cooking it with spices, meat and cashew nuts. *Lamprais* is a Dutch

Below: Negombo beach bar.

variation in which rice and curries are wrapped in banana leaves and steamed with chicken or beef, and is available at upmarket pastry shops (try the food courts at Crescat Boulevard and Majestic City, *see tour 2*).

OTHER DELIGHTS

Old Dutch and Portuguese delicacies such as *bolo fiado* (laminated cake) and *boroa* (semolina biscuits) are another element of Sri Lankan cuisine. *Biriyani*, a traditional Muslim rice-and-meat dish, and Tamil *thosai* (pancakes) and *vade* (fritters), have also become part of local cooking. *Pittu* is ground rice or plain flour mixed with coconut and then steam-cooked in a bamboo container; it is eaten with coconut milk, or with meat or fish.

A kind of flimsy pancake, *godamba roti* is a particular favourite among Muslims. It is fascinating to see this being made: with each turn of the expert handler's wrist, a small ball of flour becomes longer and flatter. Another popular dish is *watallappan*, the ingredients of which are *jaggery* (a coarse brown sugar made from the sap of the date palm), eggs, milk and cashew nuts. This is a delicious, rich dessert.

SNACKS

Indigenous snacks, known as 'short eats', are savoury bite-sized pastries or rolls, which can be bought in pastry shops to

eat there or take away. There are many types, including miniature loaves baked and stuffed with *seeni sambol*, fried pancakes with a beef, fish, chicken or vegetable filling, meat or chicken patties, and 'cutlets', deep-fried soft round balls of mashed tuna.

WHERE TO EAT

Eating in the restaurant of your hotel or guesthouse is generally a safe bet: food turnover is usually high, as are standards of freshness and hygiene. That's where you will also be able to get non-spicy dishes like grilled fish or lobster. There will always be a choice, so you don't have to be like a Sri Lankan and have curry for every meal.

Village restaurants and eateries may prove testing due to the spicy food and suspect hygiene. Unlike other Asian countries, Sri Lanka has no tradition of street food. Rest houses are usually a safe bet for local food as they are used to catering for foreign travellers as well as for their usual clientele of lawyers, government officials and sales reps. A nice custom is for drivers of guests to eat free with the staff, so don't worry about inviting your chauffeur to join you for lunch.

The best restaurants for fine dining on fusion, ethnic or continental cuisine and fast food are in Colombo. Some hotels away from the city have speciality restaurants, which offer a break from tourist food.

In recent years, private villas and small boutique hotels have opened, serving superb food but cooked only on request. However, while the restaurants of all major hotels will cater to non-resident diners, private villas normally avoid this in consideration of their guests' privacy.

DRINKS

All imported beverages (wines, spirits and beers) carry a high tax, making them very expensive. Wine, however, is easily available, with Australian, Chilean and South African all popular choices. Several locally brewed beers, like Lion Lager or Three Coins, are worth trying. For a taste of an authentic Sri Lankan product, try *arrack*. This is made from toddy (the sap of the coconut palm tree) and neutral spirit and distilled in large vats. Toddy drunk fresh from the tree is also much enjoyed by Sri Lankans, though its strong, sweaty aroma can be off-putting.

For teetotallers, there is tea, of course, as well as fruit juices, with fresh lime and soda being especially refreshing. A *thambili* (young coconut) cut open by a roadside vendor so you can drink the water within is a healthy natural beverage. Another local speciality is ginger beer made with real ginger (but make sure it's the Elephant House brand for that distinctive taste).

Above from far left: *appa* (string hoppers) are a popular accompaniment; lime and soda stall; *arrack* is the nation's favourite tipple.

Dry Days
The sale of alcohol is prohibited on *Poya* (full moon) days, even to tourists staying in hotels, and on other days according to government decree. Buy your supplies the day before.

SHOPPING

For many visitors, shopping is defined by what's available in their hotel gift shops – yet venturing out to nearby villages or making a point of shopping in Colombo or Kandy can yield more than batik sarongs and garish masks.

Opening Times
Shops usually open 10am–6pm in Colombo; in other towns, shops and supermarkets open 8am–8pm.

Sri Lanka's rich artistic traditions rival those of pretty much anywhere in the world. If you're prepared to shop around, there are excellent crafts to be found, and prices remain among the cheapest in Asia. Be careful though – many of the crafts available are of shoddy quality and stereotypical designs.

It's not just crafts on offer – tea, spices and cashew nuts can also make excellent souvenirs.

WHAT TO BUY

In Colombo, there are plenty of superior shops – such as Odel for fashions, Paradise Road for knick-knacks and Barefoot for bright fabrics – and shopping malls, like Liberty Plaza, Majestic City and the upmarket Crescat *(see tour 2)*. The other main places to buy are Kandy, which has a deluge of craft shops, and Galle, famous for its gems, jewellery, lace and Dutch antiques, and now also home to a number of designer boutiques.

Bargaining is the order of the day in smaller shops. A request for a 'small discount' or a 'special price' can sometimes work, especially if you're making a big purchase or buying several items.

Good hunting ground for shoppers, even in country towns close to resorts, is the nearest supermarket. They show what Sri Lankans buy at local prices, and staff are generally helpful.

Gems

An immense assortment of gems are to be found, with blue sapphires being the best buy. Gleaming star sapphires and star rubies are beautiful when set as rings and pendants. Alexandrites are olive-green in natural light, turning a raspberry red under artificial light. Cat's Eye, so called because it has a streak of light in the middle like the eye of a cat, comes in hues of honey-yellow and apple-green. Other popular stones are amethysts, garnets, aquamarines and moonstones.

Only buy in quality shops such as those in five-star hotels. You might find cheaper prices out of Colombo. For example, in Bentota, Aida Gems and Jewellery (192 Galle Road, Bentota; tel: 034-227 5397) has a solid reputation. Locally crafted, highly fashionable costume jewellery of exquisite design can be purchased at the Stone 'n' String outlets in Liberty Plaza, Majestic City and Crescat.

Commission Free
Gem merchants and other places selling exclusively to tourists (like spice gardens, craft shops, batik centres) build in a commission to the price they quote, so if you shop without a local guide, ask for a discount equal to the built-in commission.

Batiks

Colourful batik designs involving motifs of elephants, peacocks and Kandyan dancers make attractive sarongs, tablecloths and wall hangings. Laksala, the government handicraft shop with branches in Colombo, Kandy and Galle, stock them, as do most village markets.

Handicrafts

Craft shops stock an extensive range of items like mats, masks, drums, coconut shell dolls, porcupine-quill boxes, lace, reed, basket and bamboo-ware, lacquerware, wooden figurines, shell crafts, and silver and brassware. The varied representations of Sri Lanka's elephants, painted batik-style or carved from ebony, are attractive.

Several Colombo shops sell unique items such as cushion covers inlaid with the Sinhala or Tamil alphabet, hand-woven cotton sarongs, floating candles and colourful doorstops.

For such items, head for branches of Laksala as well as Lakmedura (113 Dharmapala Mawatha, Colombo 7, tel: 011-232 8900) and Lakpahana, (21 Rajakeeya Mawatha, Colombo 7, tel: 011-269 2554).

Tea, Spices and Cashew Nuts

Ceylon tea is Sri Lanka's most famous export. To sample the best, look for loose-leaf Orange Pekoe if you like tea without milk, or Broken Orange Pekoe for a stronger cup drunk with milk and sugar. Plantation-fresh leaf tea (avoid tea bags for a quality cup) is available at many roadside tea centres. However, for premium tea that tastes good, buy from a Mlesna outlet, or from Tea Breeze *(see tour 2)*.

Aromatic spices constitute the soul of Sri Lankan cuisine. A specialist is the Spice Shop at Majestic City, Bambalapitiya *(see tour 2)*, or try a good supermarket like Keells or Cargills.

Cashews, either plain or roasted, are sold throughout the island, in packets from shops and from stalls on street corners. Cashews are available at the Expo Shoppe in the Liberty Plaza shopping complex *(see tour 2)*. You will also find girls selling cashew nuts at Cadjugama on the road to Kandy *(see tour 6)*.

Above from far left: making batiks is an intricate process; masks and other woodcarvings in Sigiriya; gems galore.

Below: fancy a brew?

HANDUNUGODA TEA FACTORY

ENTERTAINMENT

Entertainment in Sri Lanka is lively and totally unexpected: festivals and street parades, open-air art exhibitions, Sunday brunch jazz sessions, classical and pop concerts and local comedy shows add up to a vibrant cultural scene.

Although there's not much in the way of after-dark entertainment in Sri Lanka, the country has a packed festival calendar – with spectacular processions, caparisoned elephants, and drummers and dancers aplenty – and a rich dance tradition, ranging from the flamboyant classical traditions of Kandy to the populist dance-dramas and exorcism ceremonies of the south.

DANCE AND MUSIC

The classical performing arts of Sri Lanka are generally divided into two groups: up-country, or Kandyan, encompassing the aristocratic classical dance traditions of the former Kandyan kingdom, with their lavishly costumed dancers and highly stylised choreography; and low-country, covering the much more populist traditions of the south. These feature masked *kolam* dance-dramas (usually a satirical portrayal of village life) and exorcism ceremonies, which still show strong pre-Buddhist roots and continue to be a vital part of Sri Lankan culture.

Modern Sri Lankan popular songs invariably have lyrics lamenting lost or unrequited love. Much brighter and more fun is the *baila* style inherited from the Portuguese. As well as electronic bands (and there is a flourishing heavy-metal scene), oriental groups with a harmonium and hand drums sometimes play in hotels. Sunday jazz brunch sessions are held at the Mount Lavinia Hotel *(see tour 4)*.

ART AND CINEMA

Local artists give monthly exhibitions at the Gallery Café, and the gallery at the Barefoot Café *(see tour 2)*. An art show called Kala Pola is held on the sidewalks of Ananda Coomaraswarmy Mawatha, Colombo 7, every February: over 200 artists from around the country exhibit their work for one day only.

There is a strong Sinhala-language film industry producing films for local cinemas. Liberty Cinema (Dharmapala Mawatha, Colombo 2, tel: 011-232 5264) and Majestic Cinema (Level 4, Majestic City, Bambalapitiya; tel: 011-258 1759) also regularly show new movies from Hollywood, as well as films from India. The British Council occasionally screens arthouse movies.

Magic and Fire
Major tourist hotels try to provide entertainment for their guests every night. In the Colombo five-star properties this means an electronic band playing in the lounge and a pianist in the fine-dining restaurant. Beach and hill-country hotels also have lounge-bar bands and occasionally put on shows with traditional magicians, jugglers and fire dancers.

NIGHTLIFE

If you want raucous after-dark night life, Sri Lanka isn't the place to come. Only in Colombo will you find any kind of nightlife, and even this is modest. It centres around five-star hotel discotheques, which are only occasionally open, and two favourite nightspots, both open nightly: Bistro Latino (21 De Voss Avenue, Colombo 4; tel: 011-258 0063), and Rhythm and Blues Bar (Daisy Villa Avenue, R.A. de Mel Mawatha, Colombo 4; tel: 011-5363859), which is a live music venue.

The alternative is the city's four casinos, which are open 24 hours a day, except on *Poya* days. All offer roulette, blackjack and baccarat. Drinks and snacks are available free to players, and they also offer buffet dinners and live music. Membership is in name only; anyone can sign in and play. Try Bally's Club (14 Dharmapala Mawatha, Colombo 3, tel: 011-257 3497); Bellagio (430 R.A. de Mel Mawatha, Colombo 3, tel: 011-257 5271); MGM (772 Galle Road, Colombo 4, tel: 011-259 1319); and Star Dust Club (5th Lane, Galle Road, Colombo 3, tel: 011-257 3493).

Outside the capital, the island's only after-hours activity is at the tourist resorts of Negombo, Hikkaduwa and Unawatuna, but this doesn't consist of much more than chilling out with a beer on the beach listening to Bob Marley blasting from the bar.

FESTIVALS

Peraheras (parades of elephants and dancers) are held in many places, the most popular being those in February in Colombo, Kandy in July or August and Bentota in December. The Sinhalese and Tamil New Year Festival is in mid April, when shops close and people visit their home villages, many to take part in contests like greasy pole pillow fights and bicycle races.

Not all the island's festivals are religious. Occasional kite-flying festivals are held on Galle Face Green in Colombo, and an annual surfing festival takes place in Arugam Bay, on the east coast. Hikkaduwa is home to an annual beach festival and Galle Fort hosts a literary festival in January.

Above from far left: modern art in Colombo; fire dancing is a typical hotel entertainment.

Below: performer on Negombo Beach.

SPORTS & RELAXATION

From hurtling down a river on a raft to being pampered in a herbal spa; from galloping across the sand on horseback to indulging in wellness therapy; Sri Lanka has activities for the energetic as well as pleasant ways of relaxing.

Sri Lankans are sports-conscious people. Formal sports like cricket and football would usually only engage visitors' attention as spectators, not participants; however, boys playing on village greens and on the beach would be delighted if you joined in – though don't expect an easy time.

Many sports clubs and associations accept foreign visitors as temporary members. Also, most of the major hotels have swimming pools and tennis courts.

Ayurveda

The traditional system of holistic health care known as Ayurveda (from the Sanskrit, meaning 'the science of life') has been practised in India and Sri Lanka for centuries. According to the Ayurvedic system, all bodies are made up of varying combinations of the five basic elements (ether, fire, air, earth and water) and governed by three *doshas* (*pitta*, *vata* and *kapha*). Rather than treating illnesses and symptoms in isolation, Ayurveda aims to treat the whole patient, to encourage a more balanced lifestyle.

Several resorts on the west coast provide Ayurveda therapy to alleviate medical problems, while others practise 'soft' Ayurveda to inspire well-being. Ayurveda practitioners have to be licensed by the government, and the treatment is a soothing adventure in natural wellness therapy.

CRICKET

Cricket is a national obsession in Sri Lanka, and the national team's exploits are followed religiously. The cricket season begins in September and ends with the finals in April. Visitors can enjoy the benefits of temporary membership at the Colombo Cricket Club (31 Maitland Crescent, Colombo 7; tel: 011-269 1025).

CYCLING

Although there are road races for cyclists during the mid-April Sinhalese/Tamil New Year festivities, cycling is not a regular sport. Bikes can be hired, however, at some hotels for exploring the neighbouring countryside.

DIVING AND WATERSPORTS

Underwater Safaris Ltd (25 Barnes Place, Colombo 7; tel: 011-269 4012) offers wreck- and reef-diving expeditions at Hikkaduwa on the south coast. Bentota hotels also have diving centres where equipment and boats can be hired. A range of watersports are avail-

able at some south-coast hotels and at Negombo on the west coast. At Bentota there is jet-skiing and banana-boat riding on the lagoon.

Swimming and Snorkelling

While the sea off Bentota is usually safe for swimming in season (Nov–Apr), there are dangerous currents elsewhere on the west coast. Snorkelling is possible in the rock pools below Galle Fort *(see tour 11).*

Surfing

The island's main surfing destination is Arugam Bay, with waves best from May to October and a variety of breaks suitable for novices and experts. Hikkaduwa on the west coast is best from November to April and has centres with equipment and instruction.

White-Water Rafting

This is popular at Kitulgala, on the southern edge of the hill country, where the choppy Kelani Ganga river provides boulder-strewn stretches of rapids. Check www.actionlanka.com for details of this and other adventure sports.

GOLF

Sri Lanka boasts several beautiful championship-standard golf courses, at Nuwara Eliya (tel: 052-223 833), at the Royal Colombo Golf Club (tel: 011-269 5431) and the Victoria Golf Club, Rajawella, Kandy (tel: 060-280 0249)

– and green fees are a bargain by the standards of most other countries. They all welcome temporary members.

HORSE-RIDING

There is a school attached to Heritance Ahungalla (tel: 091-555 5000; www.heritancehotels.com) for riding along the west-coast beach. Horse-riding holidays are available through the Premadasa Horseriding School (11/12 Melder Place, Nugegoda; tel: 011 282 0588; www.premadasa.lk).

SPAS

Most major hotels boast a spa facility, with treatments ranging from the basic to the exotic; you may wish to visit them first before deciding on treatment. The one at the Heritance Kandalama (tel: 066-555 5000; www.heritancehotels. com) is on the hotel's rooftop, with a superb view of the surrounding lakes and jungle. Many spas also offer Ayurveda treatment *(see feature).*

WALKING

The island's hill country *(see tours 7 and 8)* is a walker's paradise, with stunning scenery and a pleasant temperate climate. Local guides (such as Loga at Haputale, tel: 077-997 5051, and Selvam at Nuwara Eliya, tel: 077-632 6663) know the best trails in their areas, including the trek to World's End.

Above from far left: a young footballer at Negombo; exploring Sri Lanka by bike; Shirodhara, a branch of Ayurveda where a patient has oil poured onto their forehead.

Below: after-school fun in Polonnaruwa; a swim in Bentota.

HISTORY: KEY DATES

Sri Lanka's history has frequently been a violent one – though thankfully its most recent conflict, the civil war between the Liberation Tigers of Tamil Eelam (LTTE) and the Sri Lanka military, finally ended in 2009.

EARLY HISTORY

543 BC	Death of the Buddha in India and the arrival of Prince Vijaya from India with 700 followers to become the island's first king.
380 BC	The island's first capital is established at Anuradhapura.
***c.*250–210 BC**	Reign of Devanampiya Tissa. Indian Emperor Asoka sends missions to the island and converts the king and population to Buddhism.
205 BC	The Indian warrior Elara captures Anuradhapura.
161–137 BC	Elara is defeated by King Dutugemunu, and for the first time Sri Lanka is unified under a single Sinhalese monarch.
AD 993	The Cholas of South India capture Anuradhapura and the capital is moved to Polonnaruwa.

COLONIAL PERIOD

1505	The Portuguese arrive and extract concessions from the king of Kotte.
1656	The Dutch oust the Portuguese and introduce Dutch law.
1796	The Dutch surrender their possessions on the island to the British, who have become interested in Trincomalee's harbour.
1815	The last native king is captured at Kandy after the British conspire with his prime minister, ending 24 centuries of monarchy. For the first time, the whole island falls under foreign rule, becoming part of the British Empire.
1824	A revised form of government under Sir Edward Barnes and the building of roads open up the island to British settlers.
1867	Introduction of tea as a commercial crop for export coincides with the first railway line, from Colombo to Kandy to serve hill-country plantations.
1931	Universal franchise is granted.

Lost Link
The British colonial period brought about the introduction of English as a link language between the Tamils and the Sinhalese, but this link was lost when S.W.R.D Bandaranaike made Sinhala the official language. Tamils found their aspirations thwarted unless they learned Sinhala.

INDEPENDENCE

1948	Ceylon is granted independence.
1959	Prime Minister S.W.R.D. Bandaranaike assassinated by a Buddhist monk.
1960	His widow, Sirimavo Bandaranaike, becomes world's first woman prime minister.
1971	Armed rebellion by Maoist JVP in south leaves thousands dead.
1972	The country's colonial name, Ceylon, is changed to Sri Lanka.
1978	A new constitution introduces the office of executive president and brings in proportional representation. J.R. Jayewardene becomes the first president.

ETHNIC STRIFE

1983	'Black July' sees the LTTE attack on the army in the north sparking ethnic clashes. Thousands of Tamil civilians in the south are murdered by Sinhalese mobs, leading to the outbreak of civil war.
1987–8	A second JVP insurrection. Thousands more die in the south.
1989	Ranasinghe Premadasa is elected president.
1993	Premadasa is assassinated by the LTTE.
1994	Chandrika Bandaranaike Kumaratunga is elected president while her mother, Sirimavo Bandaranaike, again becomes prime minister.
1996	Sri Lanka's fledgling cricket team wins the World Cup.
1999	Chandrika Bandaranaike Kumaratunga is re-elected as president.
2004	South Asian tsunami kills more than 30,000 and leaves 100,000 homeless.
2006	Mahinda Rajapakse becomes president.
2007	The Sri Lankan army succeeds in driving the LTTE out of eastern Sri Lanka.
2009	The Sri Lankan army, led by General Sarath Fonseka, defeats the LTTE. Tiger leader Prabakaran is killed and all rebel-held territory reclaimed.
2010	Mahinda Rajapakse wins an early presidential election (while his main opponent, General Sarath Fonseka, is arrested on conspiracy charges), and his ruling coalition wins parliamentary elections.

WALKS AND TOURS

COLOMBO FORT AND PETTAH

An exciting introduction to old and new Sri Lanka, with a stroll past abandoned colonial buildings in the shadow of Colombo's modern World Trade Centre twin towers, and on to the bustling Pettah shopping district.

DISTANCE 4km (2½ miles)
TIME Half a day
START Presidential Secretariat
END World Trade Centre
POINTS TO NOTE
This tour starts and ends in the High Security Zone, where photography is prohibited; keep your camera out of sight and be prepared for any bag you are carrying to be searched. Take good care where you walk as many pavements are broken.

Tuk-Tuk Touting
The drivers of motorised rickshaws, called tuk-tuks, can't bear to see a foreigner walking; you'll need to be firm in refusing them.

Food and Drink

① CAFÉ 64
Galadari Hotel, 64 Lotus Road; tel: 011-254 4544; daily 7am–8.30pm; $
A coffee shop with a terrace, selling snacks and sandwiches (the *seeni sambol* spicy onion relish bun is delicious). A buffet lunch of curried items is served from noon to 3pm.

② PANORAMA ROOFTOP RESTAURANT
Colombo City Hotel, Level 3, 33 Canal Row; tel: 011-534 1962; daily noon–3pm, 6–11.30pm; $$
Good-value buffets and à la carte dishes like curries, or grilled fish and chicken, served in relaxed atmosphere; there is an open-air sky terrace for evening dining.

Colombo, Sri Lanka's colonial heart, is a fascinating reflection of the contrasts that define the country: from the paranoia of the High Security Zone to the friendly locals going about their daily business; from the colonnaded verandas of the past to the glitzy five-star hotels; and from the relentless traffic to the calm of municipal museums.

The **Presidential Secretariat ❶** building, formerly the parliament, with its neoclassical columns and steep steps, is the starting point for this walk. It is close to the Galadari, Ceylon Continental and Hilton hotels at the edge of the High Security Zone.

FORT

Fort, as this area is known, used to be the city's administrative and residential complex, occupied for 450 years by the Portuguese, Dutch and British in turn. Some old cannons remain by the Presidential Secretariat, but there is no trace of the old fort ramparts.

Have a coffee in **Café 64**, see ❶①, at the Galadari Hotel across the road. From there you can see, beyond the

roundabout by the sea, the promenade that runs alongside the Ceylon Continental Hotel. The road is closed, but when it reopens you could walk to the **lighthouse** built in 1951, overlooking the **Governor's Bath**, a seawater swimming pool. Beyond that is the **Jayanthi Dagoba**, a Buddhist monument dating from 1956.

King's Prison Cell

From Café 64 walk up to the security gates blocking the road to the President's House, where you can see the city's clock lighthouse in the distance. This is as far as you can walk, but look beyond the railings to see a small domed **cell ❷** with a red-tiled roof, where Sri Wickrama Rajasinghe, the

last king of Kandy (from 1798 to 1815), was imprisoned. Turn east and walk along the road that leads past the **Bank of Ceylon headquarters**.

Next to it, the glass-walled twin towers of the **World Trade Centre ❸**, Colombo's tallest and most prestigious building, loom over a colonial building opposite that was once a **Dutch Hospital**. Behind it is the **Colombo City Hotel**, which has a **Panorama Rooftop Restaurant**, see ⑪②.

President's House

After passing the World Trade Centre, turn north into York Street, past old buildings where touts lurk to introduce you to money-changers. Accept their offers at your own risk!

Above from far left: the Presidential Secretariat is overshadowed by the Galadari Hotel; getting about by tuk-tuk.

Colonial Influence
The Fort area was used as a port in the 8th century by Arab traders, and as a Portuguese settlement in the 16th century. The Dutch added many of the grand mansions that still survive; the British, who came in 1796, extended the city beyond the Fort's limits and created broad boulevards.

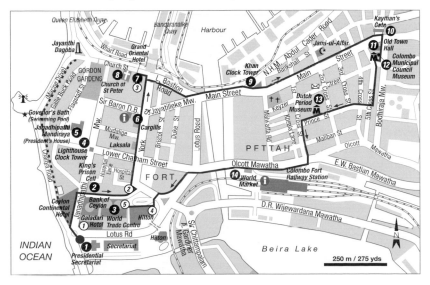

Above from left:
Cargills department
store, with the twin
towers of the World
Trade Centre behind;
signs at the Dutch
Period Museum.

Looking west, you can see the **Light-house Clock Tower** ❹ at the top of Chatham Street, but security barriers stop you getting close. Built in 1857, the lighthouse had clock faces added to its four sides in 1914. Beyond it is the **President's House** ❺, built by the last Dutch governor in the 18th century and known variously as King's or Queen's House by the British, whose governor resided in it. Hidden behind trees and in a restricted area, it is now the official home of the country's president.

Colonial Buildings
Just on the left, pop into **Laksala** (60 York Street; tel: 011-232 3513; www. laksala.lk; Mon–Sat 10am–4pm), a government-run handicraft emporium. Continuing northwards along York Street, glance up to see the puce stone walls decorated with plaster horns of plenty that herald **Cargills** ❻ (40 York Street; tel: 011-242 7777; www.cargills ceylon.com; Mon–Fri 8.15am–5.15pm), Colombo's oldest department store, established in 1844.

There's another colonial building, the **Grand Oriental Hotel** ❼, at the end of York Street by the old entrance to the port. This was built in 1837 originally as an army barracks, becoming a popular hotel for arriving ship passengers in 1875. Its copper-ceilinged **Harbour Room**, see ⑪③, is great for local buffets and to watch ships. Next to the hotel in Church Street, behind a police barricade, is the

Roads, Roads...
Sir Edward Barnes
(1776–1838), who
was governor from
1820–2 and 1824–
31, believed the way
to develop the colony
was not with fortifi-
cations but with
'roads, roads and
more roads'. His
statue stands outside
the President's House
and is the point from
which all road dis-
tances from Colombo
are measured.

Church of St Peter ❽, originally the reception and banquet hall of the Dutch governor's residence.

PETTAH

Walk eastwards in the shade of dilapi-dated colonial buildings along Leyden Bastion Road opposite the port's walls, and cross the small canal linking the harbour with the **Beira Lake**. Ahead is the **Khan Clock Tower** ❾, erected in 1923, which marks the entrance to **Pettah**. The name comes from the Tamil word *pettai* (old town). This was once a prime residential area but degenerated into 'the native quarter' as the British colonists built homes in the suburbs. Be careful of traffic as you cross Malwatta Road to walk along Main Street into the heart of Pettah.

Each of the side roads (called Cross Streets) leading south off Main Street specialises in selling different items, such as electronics or fabrics. You can take photographs, and there are plenty of colourful stalls and shops. Items are cheap since Pettah acts as a wholesaler to the nation, but unless you want a cheap mobile phone, a sari or a Chinese ornament, souvenir-shopping will be more rewarding at stores like Paradise Road and Odel *(see tour 2)*.

Municipal Mementoes
Your destination is the road's end called **Kayman's Gate** ❿; all that remains, though, is its belfry, dating from the

Dutch period. The word 'Kayman' comes from the Dutch *cayman* (crocodile) – crocodiles once gathered there to eat leftovers thrown out from Fort.

At Kayman's Gate, turn right to Bodhiraja Mawatha to see the **Old Town Hall ⑪**. Built in 1873, it is adorned with minaret-like towers and retains the double portico that once gave access to horse-drawn carriages. It is still used as municipal offices, though street stalls block its frontage.

Adjoining it is the open-sided **Colombo Municipal Council Museum ⑫** (Bodhiraja Mawatha; Mon–Sat 7.30am–6pm; free), where the exhibits include early 20th-century steamrollers and the granite slab commemorating the bequeathing of Galle Face promenade to Colombo.

Dutch Period Museum

Now dive south down 5th Cross Street to turn west into Prince Street, crowded with shops selling glass and mirrors. The old post office here was restored in 1980 as the **Dutch Period Museum ⑬** (tel: 011-244 8466; Sat–Thur 9am–5pm; charge), filled with colonial furniture and household items.

Leaving the museum, turn south down 1st Cross Street to emerge in the frenzy of Olcott Mawatha in front of **Fort railway station**, the country's main rail terminal. The road is named after an American Buddhist crusader, Henry Steel Olcott (1832–1907), whose statue stands in the station car park.

World Market

Adjoining the station, the **World Market ⑭** is open throughout the day and early evening. Mainly suit, shirt and dress materials are sold here, and bargaining is expected.

By now you'll need a rest. Continue west and cross Lotus Road to pop into the Hilton Hotel's **Spices** restaurant, see ⑪④, for a huge buffet lunch. Or a smart, lower-cost option for a snack is **Barista**, see ⑪⑤, a coffee shop in the World Trade Centre, reached by an escalator from the northern corner of the Hilton's forecourt. Be prepared for another security check – you are back in the city's High Security Zone.

Food and Drink

③ HARBOUR ROOM

Grand Oriental Hotel, 2 York Street; tel: 011-232 0320; daily 12.30–3pm, 7.30–11.30pm; $$

On weekdays, a rice and curry buffet lunch, popular with city executives, is served in this magnificent dining room with a harbour view. On Friday and Saturday evening is an international buffet, and on Sunday, a low-priced à la carte menu.

④ SPICES

Lobby level, Colombo Hilton, 2 Sir Chittampalam A. Gardiner Mawatha; tel: 011-249 2492; daily noon–2.30pm, 7–11pm; $$$

Very popular for either a quick lunch, with an extensive range of dishes (not necessarily spicy, and with Western roasts too), or a more leisurely dinner, when a grander array of international dishes is on offer.

⑤ BARISTA

Level 3, World Trade Centre (WTC), Echelon Square; tel: 011-239 4784; Mon–Fri 8am–6pm; $

Dedicated to good coffee and quick snacks, with a bookshop at its entrance, this place gets busy with office workers.

COLOMBO CITY SIGHTS

Hire an air-conditioned taxi or a tuk-tuk for this exciting morning drive around Colombo, which provides a fascinating introduction to the religion and culture that define the country, and bags of shopping opportunities.

DISTANCE 25km (15½ miles)
TIME Half a day
START Galle Face Hotel
END Cinnamon Grand Hotel
POINTS TO NOTE

While hotel taxis have printed price lists, the fare for a three-wheeler taxi (tuk-tuk) needs to be negotiated before setting off. To get an idea of what to pay, check the hotel taxi printed rates first, then ask a few tuk-tuk drivers separately (so they don't collude to quote the same price) for quotations to find an acceptable fare. Sometimes the hotel taxi fixed fee will be cheaper for the morning's hire than a tuk-tuk. Taxis and tuk-tuks will wait while you sightsee or shop. A tip of about 5 percent of the fare for a hotel taxi or an extra Rs20 for the tuk-tuk driver should be sufficient.

Shops in Colombo open from 10am, so don't start this tour too early if you plan to shop. Supermarkets and department stores (but not all outlets in the shopping malls) are open on Sundays too.

Temple Offerings

At the Gangaramaya museum, feast your eyes on shelves chock-a-block with sandalwood and ivory carvings, brass statues and even old fountain pens and eyeglasses, strewn between jade, crystal and ivory ornaments, presented to the temple as offerings. There is also a collection of elephant tusks and vintage cars. The resident guide will be disappointed if you aren't astonished.

From Fort, Colombo stretches southwards down the west coast to the commercial suburbs of Colpetty (Kollupitiya) and Bambalapitiya, and bulges eastwards inland to Slave Island (Kompannavidiya), the compound for slaves in Dutch times, the broad avenues of upscale residential area Cinnamon Gardens, and on to the parliamentary capital of Sri Jayawardenapura-Kotte. This tour offers a comfortable view of the landmarks and green spaces of Colombo, famous in the 1920s as Asia's Garden City.

GALLE FACE GREEN

Start this tour at one of Colombo's oldest and most traditional hotels, the **Galle Face ❶** (established 1864), worth a visit for breakfast on the patio of its **Veranda Café**, see ⑪①, or to relax on the front veranda with its view of **Galle Face Green**, formerly a racecourse.

Then drive south down Galle Road to call in at the information desk of the **Sri Lanka Tourism Promotion Bureau** (80 Galle Road; tel: 011-243 7055; Mon–Fri 8.30am–4.15pm). This is on the seaside just before **Temple Trees ❷** (the official residence of the

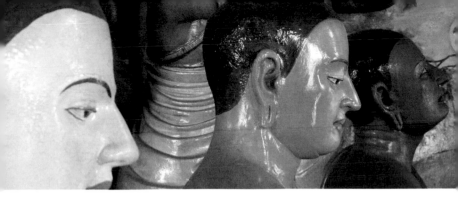

prime minister), which is opposite on the land side. Turn inland at the Kollupitiya junction and pass **Bally's** (14 Dharmapala Mawatha, Colombo 3; tel: 011-257 3497), one of Colombo's four 24-hour casinos, on the right before the **Liberty Plaza** shopping mall, good for DVDs and cheap imported goods.

COLOMBO CITY

At the roundabout by Liberty Plaza, take the main road (Dharmapala Mawatha) inland. If you fancy a cup of pure Ceylon tea, stop at **Tea Breeze**, see ⑪②, on the first floor of a glass-fronted building 200m/yds along the road.

Gangaramaya Temple

At the next junction, turn northwards (left) into Sir James Peiris Mawatha to see the inspiring sight of the **Seema Malakaya ❸** assembly hall for monks (daily 8.30am–6pm; donation), perched on an island in the serene waters of **Beira Lake**. You can park there, then walk across to it on a narrow wooden bridge. The late 20th-century assembly hall, designed by the late trendsetting architect Geoffrey Bawa, is part of the **Gangaramaya Temple ❹** (tel: 011-232 7084; www.gangaramaya.com; daily 6am–10pm; donation).

Visit Gangaramaya as you drive back to Dharmapala Mawatha, by taking Sri Jinarathana Road eastwards. Old railway carriages are parked on the pavement opposite this Buddhist temple and an elephant resides in the compound. It houses a bizarre **museum** (daily 9am–6pm; charge) of items presented by devotees. In February, the area takes on a festive air when the Navam Perahera (procession) fills the streets.

Vihara Mahadevi Park and the Town Hall

Back on Dharmapala Mawatha, heading east, the green lawns and shady trees of **Vihara Mahadevi Park ❺** are all that remain of what was once a vast garden of cinnamon trees – the area is still known as Cinnamon Gardens. The park fronts an impressive building resembling a miniature version of the Capitol building in Washington, DC. This is the **Town Hall ❻**, and it is best admired from the **balcony café**, see ⑪③ *(p.35)*, of the **Paradise Road** store – an Aladdin's cave of unusual souvenirs

---

Food and Drink

① VERANDA CAFÉ
Galle Face Hotel, 2 Galle Road; tel: 011-254 1010; www.gallefacehotel.com; daily 7.30–9.30am, 12.30–2.30pm, 7.30–10.30pm; $$
Local and international buffets are served on the veranda overlooking the garden patio of Colombo's venerable seaside hotel, with a colonial atmosphere and courteous staff.

② TEA BREEZE
68A Dharmapala Mawatha; tel: 011-266 7711; www.mackwoodstea.com; daily 10am–8pm; $
With a floor-to-ceiling glass wall, this first-floor café affords a panoramic view while you sip pure estate-fresh Ceylon tea and enjoy delicious cakes and sandwiches.

from tropical candles to faux-Victorian toys. By **De Soysa Circus** (formerly Lipton's Circus), at the end of the road, is another store, **Odel**, selling designer clothes at cheaper prices than in Europe. There is a sushi bar, **Nihon-bashi**, see ⑪④, inside.

COLOMBO SUBURBS

Find your waiting vehicle for a drive south down C.W.W. Kannangara Road, past the minarets of the old **Devatagaha Mosque**, then turn eastwards (right) into Horton Place. This

Kelaniya Temple

Consider a visit to Kelaniya Rajamaha Vihara Temple, 11km (7 miles) north of Colombo. Drive east from Colombo Fort and turn right after crossing the Kelaniya Bridge; then right soon after Peliyagoda for the road leading to the temple, which is more than 2,500 years old. Be sure to see the two statues of the Buddha and the extraordinary frescoes depicting the Buddha's life and important events in the island's history.

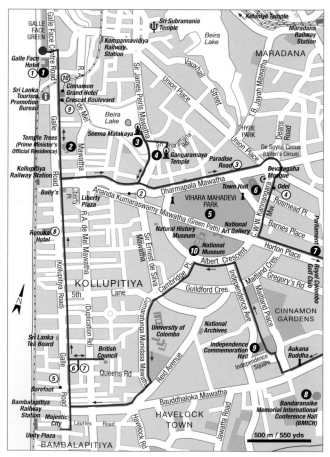

sweeps through a residential area of fine houses and links up with the boulevard called Sri Jayewardenepura Mawatha.

New Parliament

Take this for 10km (6 miles) to the island's nominal new capital, **Sri Jayewardenepura-Kotte**, to get a view (no visitors allowed) of the Bawa-designed **Parliament** ❼, built in Kandyan style with tall pillars and sweeping roofs, and poised as if floating in the middle of the Diyawanna Lake.

Kotte was one of Sri Lanka's ancient capitals, and the king was in residence here when the Portuguese, the first invaders from Europe to colonise the island, arrived in 1505.

Convention Centre

On the southern side of the boulevard as you return to the city is Colombo's 18-hole **golf course** (Royal Colombo Golf Club, 223 Ven Pelpola Vipassi Himi Mawatha (formerly Model Farm Road); tel: 011-269 5431), where visitors can play for a fee. Drive past Kanatta Cemetery and at the roundabout turn into Bauddhaloka Mawatha. About 1km (½ mile) down this road on the left is the grandiose **Bandaranaike Memorial International Conference Hall** ❽ (BMICH; Bauddhaloka Mawatha; tel: 011-269 1131). The octagonal building was a gift from the Chinese government to Sri Lanka in memory of the assassinated prime minister S.W.R.D.

Bandaranaike (1899–1959). Close to its entrance is a 1970s replica of the **Aukana Buddha Statue** – the original at Aukana, in the island's interior, was carved out of sheer rock sometime around AD 400.

Next, turn right into the first road (Maitland Place) after the BMICH, then left into Independence Square to see the **Independence Commemoration Hall** ❾. Built in the style of an ancient Kandyan audience hall, it was erected shortly after Sri Lanka gained independence from Britain in 1948.

NATIONAL MUSEUM

Independence Avenue, leading from the square, links up with Albert Crescent. The grand Victorian building there is the **Colombo National Museum** ❿ (Sat–Thur 9am–5pm; tel: 011-269 4767; charge), with a varied collection ranging from Buddhist

Above from far left: a crowd outside the BMICH; a decorative ceiling in the Gangaramaya Temple; one of the Hindu bronzes in the National Museum.

Road Sense
Many of Colombo's streets have been changed from dual traffic to one-way, and some roads are closed occasionally, so be patient when you discover you have to negotiate an unexpected diversion.

Food and Drink 🍴

③ PARADISE ROAD CAFÉ
213 Dharmapala Mawatha; tel: 011-268 6043; www.paradiseroadsl.com; daily 10am–7pm; $$
Set on the tiny balcony of the Paradise Road emporium of good taste and unusual souvenirs, this café serves good coffee and delicious cakes in a refined ambience.

④ NIHONBASHI
Odel, ground floor, Alexandra Place; tel: 011-471 8758; www.nihonbashi.lk; daily noon–8pm; $$
Sushi bar and small restaurant in the Odel department store, perfect for a light lunch and fine Japanese dishes during a break from shopping.

Above from left: the National Museum's imposing exterior; inside Fort Railway Station.

statues and royal regalia to kitchen utensils and antique puppets. Return to the waiting vehicle for a drive via Cambridge Place and Cumaratunga Munidasa Mawatha, past the playing fields and campus of Colombo University, to rejoin Bauddhaloka Mawatha.

RETAIL THERAPY

Where this road joins the Galle Road, you can detour 50m/yds southwards to Bambalapitiya to visit the **Majestic City** shopping mall, great for fashions and electronics. **Unity Plaza**, the building next to it, has the well-stocked Vijitha Yapa Bookshop (tel: 011-259 6960; daily 9.30am–6pm) and a host of computer stores. If you turn north instead, **Barefoot** (704 Galle Road; tel: 011-250 2467; Mon–Sat 10am–7pm, Sun 11am–5pm), with colourful hand-loom fabrics and a **garden café**, see ⑪⑤, is on the seaside. Drive further on and turn right into Alfred House Gardens. This leads to the **British Council**, with its fine, free library.

Lunch Options

To the right, in Alfred House Road, is the **Gallery Café**, see ⑪⑥, while opposite is the **Cricket Club Café**, see ⑪⑦. Another option is to continue along the Galle Road to the Renuka Hotel with its **Palmyrah Restaurant**, see ⑪⑧. The final stop is the **Crescat Boulevard**, part of the **Cinnamon Grand Hotel** complex. As well as stylish shops, Crescat has a basement food court, see ⑪⑨. If seafood takes your fancy, the hotel's **Lagoon Restaurant**, see ⑪⑩, serves up a feast.

Food and Drink

⑤ BAREFOOT CAFÉ
704 Galle Road; tel: 011-258 9305; daily 10am–10pm; $$
In a garden behind the Barefoot store, the café serves salads and fusion-style food for lunch and dinner, as well as innovative snacks, in a bright tropical atmosphere.

⑥ GALLERY CAFÉ
2 Alfred House Road, off Alfred House Gardens; tel: 011-258 2162; daily 11am–11pm; $$$
The place for Colombo's café society to be seen, relaxing in the flagstone garden or savouring exquisite dishes like steak with fresh rosemary in the open-sided dining pavilion.

⑦ CRICKET CLUB CAFÉ
34 Queens Road (off Duplication Road); tel: 011-250 1384; www.thecricketclubcafeceylon.com; daily 11am–11pm; $$
Cricket is the theme here, with memorabilia on the walls and quickly served dishes like spinach salad and lamb pie named after famous players.

⑧ PALMYRAH RESTAURANT
Renuka Hotel, 328 Galle Road; tel: 011-257 3598; daily 11am–2pm, 6–11pm; $$
Refined local cuisine with a northern Sri Lanka influence, as well as individually prepared Western dishes; very popular with Sri Lankans and visitors alike.

⑨ CRESCAT FOOD COURT
Crescat Boulevard, 89 Galle Road; tel: 011-256 4238; daily 11am–10.30pm; $
Asian cuisine and Western fare at this self-service basement food court, attracting a young, upmarket crowd.

⑩ LAGOON
Cinnamon Grand Hotel, 77 Galle Road; tel: 011-243 7437; daily noon–3pm, 7–11pm; $$$
At this lively restaurant by the hotel's garden fish pond, you choose from an abundance of fish and seafood, then have it cooked how you like and served with a choice of sauces.

KELANI VALLEY
RAIL JOURNEY

*This tour by quaint passenger train, through the cluttered suburbs of
Colombo to the verdant paddy fields marking the beginning of Sri Lanka's
rural interior, reveals glimpses of the country that tourists seldom see.*

Train travel arrived in what was then Ceylon with the opening of a single broad-gauge line to Kandy in 1867. With the transportation of the country's new crop, tea, from the hill country to Colombo's port, the rail prospered, resulting in a network covering the whole country. A single-track, narrow-gauge line was laid from Colombo through the Kelani Valley via Homagama to Avissawella in 1902.

In 1991, still served by a diminutive steam locomotive built in 1924, the line underwent improvements. A broad-gauge line was created, and the steam engine and its wooden carriages were scrapped. Diesel-hauled carriages now run on the Kelani Valley (KV) Line, ferrying commuters to and from Colombo. This is a wonderful, unusual tour for rail buffs and tourists who want to encounter ordinary Sri Lankans going about their daily routine.

FORT RAILWAY STATION

Ticket kiosk number 14 at **Fort railway station** ❶ opens at 8.15am, 30 minutes before the departure of Train Number

DISTANCE 25km (15½ miles)
TIME 1½ hours (or 2½ hours including return by road)
START Colombo Fort Railway Station
END Homagama
POINTS TO NOTE
Train times can change, so check the current timetable before going to Fort station, either by telephone (011-243 4215) or at www.railway.gov.lk. If possible take this tour on a Wednesday, which is market day in Homagama.

9254 for Avissawella. If that's too early, there is another train, Number 9260, leaving at 1.55pm. The kiosk is at the northern end of the station forecourt, on the right as you approach the station from the main road.

Fort station is the starting point for trains bound for Kandy, the north and the hill country. It has an old-fashioned ambience, with a wooden-faced awning stretching its length. Hanging outside

Restaurant Car
One of the narrow wooden passenger carriages from the KV Line has been preserved as a restaurant at the Heritance Tea Factory Hotel near Nuwara Eliya (see tour 7).

Above: departure board; a train pulls into the station.

the stationmaster's office on platform 3 are antique wooden frames containing views of the railway from bygone days.

Steam Locomotive

After buying your ticket, enter the station on platform 3 where, in the morning, the **Udarata Menike** is parked ready to leave for Kandy and the hill country. This is likely to be the train that the few tourists gathered at the station are catching.

Cross over the footbridge at the northern end of the platform to the island platform 10/11. In the yard outside a brightly painted **steam locomotive** is on display. The train leaves from one side of this platform – usually a few minutes late, once freight has been loaded into the guard's van.

MARADANA STATION

Since only locals usually use this train, the signs painted on the interior of the carriage are in Sinhala. One requests

'no smoking', but travellers ignore it. The windows and doors are left open for the breeze to blow in, and are only closed when it is raining.

As the train sets off, look through a window on the right, as you face the engine, to see another steam engine stabled in lonely splendour in a building in the railway marshalling yard. On the other side of the tracks, abandoned rolling stock peeps from vegetation while a small shunting engine putters around like a ghost from the past.

The train jerks into **Maradana station**, which has kept its original colonial ambience and railway furniture. Drivers and guards exchange gossip while more freight is loaded. As there is no lavatory on the train, the station toilet here is your last chance until the destination. The driver sounds a horn to signal departure, and the train runs along the outermost of several lines until it veers off to the right on the single line that runs down a narrow funnel formed by two side walls overhung by trees.

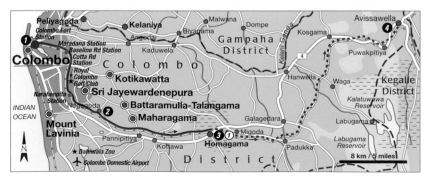

ROYAL COLOMBO GOLF CLUB

You're now passing through the backside of Colombo's crowded suburbs, where the rear doors and windows of ramshackle terraced houses open onto the line. You might want to shake hands with the people who have gathered up their laundry from where it was drying on the line and are waiting for the train to pass. Be careful not to lean out, though, in case you get caught on an overhanging roof.

More passengers get on at the suburban stations of **Baseline Road** and **Cotta Road**. Then the train suddenly breaks free of the shacks hemming in the line and emerges into a patch of bright, well-kept lawns and flower-filled ponds: the **Royal Colombo Golf Club** *(see p. 35)*. Play stops as the train ambles across the fairways and golfers watch it with bemusement.

NUGEGODA

At the next station, **Narahenpita**, more passengers get on, only to leave the train at busy **Nugegoda** ❷, the Colombo suburb where many private hospitals are located. In this more prosperous area, vegetation lines the track instead of shacks.

The wheels begin to sing shrilly as the train speeds up and follows tight curves to enter open country. Plantain, mango, breadfruit and coconut palm trees begin to crowd in on the line, while beyond them bright-green paddy fields glisten in the distance.

HOMAGAMA

The air seems hill-country fresh as the train pulls into **Homagama** ❸, a busy village marking the entrance to Sri Lanka's rural interior. As you alight, the stationmaster hands the driver the token that means the line is clear to continue. Surrender your ticket at the gate and turn right to walk up to the main road where tuk-tuks are parked.

You can hire one of these for the ride along the **High Level Road** back to Colombo. Before you set out, stop for much-needed refreshment at the **Bonn Bonn Guesthouse**, see ⑪①, about 200m/yds along the High Level Road behind Homagama Police Station.

Alternatively, you could stay on the train all the way to **Avissawella** ❹, 35km (22 miles) further inland

Above from far left: just the ticket; train travellers; going round the bend.

Food and Drink 🍴

① BONN BONN GUESTHOUSE
Homagama; tel: 011-289 2606; restaurant daily 6am–11pm, bar daily 10am–11pm; 20 AC rooms; $
Hidden down a lane beside the Homagama Police Station, this recently built guesthouse has a veranda for low-priced snacks, like devilled chicken, and drinks, with a view of its sparkling swimming pool and surrounding woodland.

Private Care
The medical care at Colombo's private hospitals, centred around Nugegoda, is excellent and inexpensive, if a little informal (visitors are allowed at any time), and some tourists visit Sri Lanka specifically for medical treatment in private hospital rooms furnished like hotels.

MOUNT LAVINIA
AND DEHIWALA ZOO

For a pleasant day's break from Colombo, this tour takes in a morning relaxing on the beach, an alfresco lunch and an afternoon stroll through the lush National Zoological Gardens.

DISTANCE 15km (9 miles)
TIME A full day
START Colombo
END Dehiwala Zoo
POINTS TO NOTE
While the public beach alongside it is free, there is a charge for non-resident guests to use the beach facilities at the Mount Lavinia Hotel. Foreigners visiting the zoo are charged 20 times more than Sri Lankans for admission, but there's no exclusivity or special facilities in return for paying extra.

Safe Swimming
Swimming from Mount Lavinia Beach is safe and very popular, but make sure someone you know guards your belongings, otherwise you might not have any when you return from the sea.

If your visit to Sri Lanka is too short for you to relax on the broad, and more peaceful, west-coast beaches further south, then the strand of sand at Mount Lavinia will give you a sample of Sri Lanka's beach life. The beach here is busier than those further south at Bentota and Hikkaduwa and it has a more raffish air to it too as locals play beach games, swim, and dive into the shack-style snack bars. It has the additional attraction of being within easy reach of the Dehiwala Zoo, for an enjoyable afternoon stroll in the tree-shaded park that forms the zoo.

The drive south from Colombo is along the busy Galle Road, with gleaming new shop frontages beside dilapidated general stores, and noisy buses and cars competing for space as they weave in and out of the traffic lanes. The steep new flyover (built with British aid) at the **Dehiwala Junction** provides glimpses into second-floor apartment windows, adding to the novelty of the drive. Allow more time than you expect for the 10km (6-mile) drive from the city centre because of heavy, slow-moving traffic.

MOUNT LAVINIA BEACH

The turn-off to **Mount Lavinia Beach** is about 1km (½ mile) south after the town's General Cemetery (which is on the seaside). Look for the signs advertising beach restaurants where the road forks and leave the Galle Road there, taking the southwest prong to go down Hotel Road. Drive or walk down any road to the west off Hotel Road to access the beach. You'll cross a web of rail tracks, so watch out for trains as there is no marked crossing point.

Mount Lavinia Hotel

By continuing to the end of Hotel Road you will reach the **Mount Lavinia Hotel ❶**. The railway station adjoins it, so if you come by train, you could walk northwards along the road or the beach to the hotel.

As Sri Lanka's premier heritage hotel, the Mount Lavinia sits grandly atop the small promontory that juts out to sea, separating the public beach from the more sedate hotel beach (open daily to non-residents; charge). This sprawling hotel has grown up around a 200-year-old colonial villa, originally the retreat of Governor Thomas Maitland who, legend has it, entertained his local mistress (Lavinia) here. It maintains a colonial charm and offers a variety of splendid lunch options after a morning on the beach, whether it's a snack on the poolside veranda or à la carte lunch at the **Governor's Restaurant**, see ❶①.

Beach Life

The beach to the north of the hotel stretches in patches right up to Colombo, but the broad expanse of sand that borders the hotel's northern wing is the city's most popular. Here are several restaurants of differing standard;

Above from far left:
Mount Lavinia Beach, with palm trees, sea and sand.

Food and Drink

① GOVERNOR'S RESTAURANT
Mount Lavinia Hotel, 100 Hotel Road, Mount Lavinia; tel: 011 271 5221; www.mountlaviniahotel.com; daily 12.30–3pm, 7–10.30pm; $$$$
Managed by a Sri Lankan former chef of international repute, the Mount Lavinia Hotel's restaurant features both traditional 'slow-cooked' food like citric glazed quail and molecular cuisine like exotic pheasant extract, enjoyed in a quasi-colonial ambience. Great for entertaining friends who are gourmets.

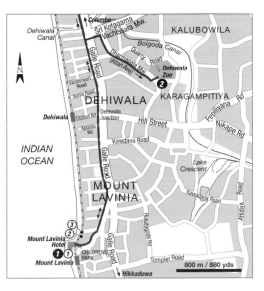

Above from left:
a pair of leopards at
Dehiwala Zoo; brightly
coloured post boxes
in Negombo.

recommended are the **Golden Mile**, see
🍴②, built out of timber like a lookout
platform, and the thatched open-sided
pavilion **Loon Tao**, see 🍴③. The beach
is equally popular for alfresco dining
and impromptu parties at night.

DEHIWALA ZOO

After a fabulous beachside lunch, a
tuk-tuk will take you to the **Dehiwala
Zoo ❷** (tel: 011-371 2751; www.
colombozoo.gov.lk; daily 8.30am–6pm;
charge) by returning northwards along
the Galle Road and back over the Dehiwala flyover. After 1 km (½ mile), turn
inland at Dharmapala Mawatha (formerly Allan Avenue) to reach the zoo.

Officially known as the National
Zoological Gardens, this is a spectacular spread of gardens, waterfalls, ponds,
shaded walks, and animals from all over
the world. Begun by John Hargenberg
as a depot for exporting animals, the
zoo was taken over by the government
in 1936 and now covers 10 hectares (24
acres). There are approximately 350
species and about 3,500 animals.
Arrows clearly indicate the direction to
follow from the entrance to make a
circular tour to see the whole zoo.

The Animals
The zoo pioneered the policy of
placing animals in an artificial habitat,
rather than simply displaying them in
cages. Here lions, bears, tigers, rhinos,
giraffes and gorillas all benefit from a
relatively high degree of freedom.

In the **Reptile House** you will find
a rare albino cobra. Watch out for the
little tortoises that ride piggyback on
ferocious crocodiles. Don't miss the
500 varieties of marine life at the **Mini
Medura** (aquarium), which is ideal for
children. The **Nocturnal House**
allows visitors to see night creatures
such as owls and lemurs in their natural habitat. The zoo also has an
excellent collection of primates.

During an afternoon visit you can see
animals being fed from 3pm, and also
hear talks about elephants, chimpanzees
and sea lions. On weekends and public
holidays there are elephant and pony
rides (2.30–4pm). It is prudent to escape
the crowds and leave the zoo an hour or
so before it is due to close, to catch a
three-wheeler back to Colombo.

Food and Drink 🍴

② GOLDEN MILE
43/14 Mount Beach, off College Avenue, Mount Lavinia; tel:
011-273 3997; www.jaysonsholdings.com; daily 11am–
midnight; $$$
Huge portions of fresh seafood and grilled meat dishes
served either in its fenced beach compound or upstairs on a
deck of timber with rugged wooden furniture and a fine view.
Friendly service and a well-stocked bar make for a good time.

③ LOON TAO
43/12 College Avenue, Mount Lavinia; tel: 011-272 2723;
daily 11am–3pm, 6–11pm; $$
Pull up in the restaurant's own car park in College Avenue
and walk down the road, across the rail track, and north
along the beach for 100m/yds to enjoy Chinese seafood for a
quiet lunch, or a more lively ambience at night. Free corkage.

NEGOMBO VIA THE WETLANDS

After driving though the industrial suburbs north of Colombo, discover an enchanting wetland wilderness on the way to the beach resort of Negombo during a day of exhilarating contrasts.

One of the largest towns along the west coast, Negombo rose to prominence during the colonial era thanks to its abundant supplies of wild cinnamon. The centre of the town preserves a few reminders of the Dutch period, including the remains of an old fort (converted by the British into a prison and still used as such), a ramshackle old rest house, and the Dutch canal, which arrows due north from Negombo to Puttalam, over 100km (62 miles) away.

Midway between Colombo and Negombo, the beautiful wetlands of Muthurajawela offer a tranquil escape from the surrounding urban sprawl.

MUTHURAJAWELA

Leave Colombo at 6am if you want to take the first boat tour of the day and see marsh bird life at its best at the Muthurajawela Wetlands. The first boat leaves at 7.30am but later trips can be arranged. Telephone in advance, anyway, to check there is a boat available.

As you drive out of Colombo on the A3, which is the main highway to the airport, it seems difficult to believe that

> **DISTANCE** 40km (25 miles)
> **TIME** A leisurely day
> **START** Colombo
> **END** Negombo
> **POINTS TO NOTE**
> This is a fascinating tour with which to conclude a visit to Sri Lanka, since it gives an insight into the island's diverse scenery and bird life, and allows time at Negombo – the liveliest beach resort, and the closest one to the airport.

Cinnamon

One of Sri Lanka's most attractive commodities, in the eyes of the Dutch, was the plentiful cinnamon that grew wild in the jungles there. It was in huge demand in Europe, where it was valued for its distinctive flavour and aid to digestion. Cinnamon found in the Negombo area was regarded as the sweetest, and hence the most highly prized.

Cinnamon was so valuable that it was made a capital offence to damage plants or to trade it illegally. However, Arab traders were more familiar than Dutch naval patrols with the Negombo coast, so smuggling cinnamon was as lucrative for them as it was when sold legally by the Dutch.

Boat Trip
The Karavas are famous for their fleets of distinctive *oruva* boats, small canoes with a pair of wooden floats and topped by a huge square sail. Short trips on an *oruva* on the lagoon, or boat trips along the old Dutch canal, can be arranged.

Below: the little egret; monkeying around.

an ecological haven could be found anywhere near the cacophony of traffic or factory yards and container terminals. After passing through the busy town of **Ja-Ela**, turn off the A3, west towards the sea at the Tudella junction. There is a large sign there, but it is in Sinhala. About 3km (2 miles) after passing a container yard you come to Bopitiya town. Don't turn off there, but keep driving straight ahead for another 500m/yds and watch carefully for a sign with the words 'The Marsh' indicating a lane on the left side of the road. The rest of the sign is in Sinhala.

Wetlands
The lane continues for another 500m/yds alongside the Hamilton Canal to the **Muthurajawela Wetlands ❶** (Bopitiya, Pamunugama; tel: 011-483 0150; daily 7.30am–4pm; charge). The compound of thatched huts you see is the visitor centre, where open boats wait for visitors. It is a state-run institution staffed by young and knowledgeable nature-lovers, not freelance tourist guides. The full programme includes a talk on the ecology of the Wetlands and a documentary. Refreshments can also be arranged.

The saltwater wetlands and lagoons are home to abundant bird life as well as to toque macaque monkeys, water monitors and the occasional crocodile. The boat putters down the Hamilton Canal before reaching the southern end of the Negombo Lagoon, a breezy expanse of water running around patches of tangled mangrove swamp with egrets, herons and kingfishers perched in the branches.

NEGOMBO
After this enchanting boat ride, return to the A3 to head northwards past **Seeduwa** and the turn-off to the **Colombo International Airport**. Continue down a wide dual carriageway and after 5km (3 miles), turn west where a sign indicates 1.85km to Beach Road, **Negombo ❷**. The railway line is on one side and shops are on the other as you head into the busy town.

St Mary's Church
In the middle of town stands the stately pink landmark of **St Mary's Church**, one of the many large Roman Catholic churches that dot Negombo and the coast north from Colombo. Portuguese missionaries were particularly active in the area, converting many of the local Karava fishermen. Their devotion to Roman Catholicism can still be seen, not only in the churches, but also in the dozens of beautiful little wayside shrines along the main roads around town.

A detour towards the sea runs past the harbour, fish-market area and St Mary's College, before emerging into Lewis Place with its guesthouses. Continue along Lewis Place to Poruthota Road, **Ettukala**, north of the town, for the main beach and hotel area.

Negombo Beach

After leaving your vehicle in Poruthota Road (or one of the side roads leading inland), it's a pleasant stroll along this main street. The beach is blocked off from the road by the hotels lining the shore, so you might have to walk through a hotel lobby to reach it. This is a working beach, the preserve of fishermen mending their nets, making reed baskets or working on their vessels in preparation for the night's fishing.

Lunch Options

If you stay the night, you'll find this is when Negombo comes to life, with its strip of bars and restaurants on both sides of Poruthota Road. Renowned for its fresh seafood, **Oysters**, see ⑪①, is easily recognisable by the huge bougainvillea tree that shades it. Lunch is also available freshly cooked on demand. Other places to eat on the strip include **Pub 4x4 International**, see ⑪②, and **Lords**, see ⑪③.

The town is blessed with a variety of low-priced guesthouses, many run by foreigners, mass-market hotels and a top, boutique-style hostelry, **The Beach**. It is a lively, slightly edgy town, and, thanks in part to the cocktail bars and innovative restaurants that are lacking elsewhere in the island, ideal for finishing a holiday in Sri Lanka.

Above from far left:
Negombo port, with an *oruva* boat in the background; family fun on Negombo Beach.

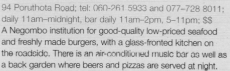

Food and Drink

① OYSTERS RESTAURANT & BAR

94 Poruthota Road; tel: 060-261 5933 and 077-728 8011; daily 11am–midnight, bar daily 11am–2pm, 5–11pm; $$
A Negombo institution for good-quality low-priced seafood and freshly made burgers, with a glass-fronted kitchen on the roadside. There is an air-conditioned music bar as well as a back garden where beers and pizzas are served at night.

② PUB 4X4 INTERNATIONAL

74 Poruthota Road; tel: 031-487 4900; daily 11am–11pm; $
With quad bikes as decor, this pub, also known as George's Dining Bar and Grill, part of the Sherryland complex, serves daily specials such as prawn chow mein and grilled paraw fish for lunch to guests who sit perched on stone benches.

③ LORDS

80B Poruthota Road; tel: 077-723 4721; www.lords restaurant.net; daily 10.30am–11pm; $$
Guests dine beside a pond of catfish in this open-sided British restaurant, bar and art gallery, on variations of sea-food dishes such as crab in white wine and cheese sauce. It gets very lively at night.

6
ELEPHANT ORPHANAGE AND KANDY

Journey through pineapple country, a cashew-nut market and a cane-weaving village to drop in at the world's only elephant orphanage before driving up to Sri Lanka's former royal capital, Kandy, to visit the revered Temple of the Tooth.

DISTANCE 116km (72 miles)
TIME Two days
START Colombo
END Kandy
POINTS TO NOTE

Although the distance may seem short, this tour is better spread over two days, as there is so much to see and do. This tour can precede tour 7 to Nuwara Eliya and the hill country, or alternatively tours 9 and 10, taking in the ancient capitals of Anuradhapura and Polonnaruwa. From there, a tour to Trincomalee and the east-coast beaches could be included.

Take the Train
An intercity express train with seats that can be booked in advance leaves Colombo Fort station at 6.40am every morning and arrives in Kandy at 9.10am. The return express leaves Kandy at 3pm and arrives in Colombo at 5.30pm.

The road to Kandy is a fascinating one, thanks to the insight it provides into rural Sri Lanka and its Buddhist culture. On this two-day tour you can explore two botanical gardens, feed baby elephants, enjoy an energetic evening dance performance, discover a forgotten rococo fountain and stroll alongside a huge king-made lake.

Until the British conquest, Kandy was the citadel of power for Sri Lankan kings. The original road there was built in 1820, piercing a wall of rock that had previously prevented the kingdom from being invaded. Now, as the A1, it is a modern highway – although heavy traffic and the sights along the way mean the drive from Colombo to Kandy could take over four hours.

HENERATHGODA BOTANICAL GARDENS

Check out of your **Colombo** hotel after breakfast and settle down for a drive of amazing contrasts by taking the Kandy Road at the Kelani Bridge. Some 25km (15½ miles) from Colombo, near **Yakkala**, stalls selling the sweetest pineapples in the country line the roadside. Buy them whole, or in pieces sprinkled with chilli powder as a spicy snack.

Turn off the Kandy Road at the 27km (17-mile) marker at **Miriswatta** to make a detour for 4km (2½ miles) down the B288 road signposted to **Gampaha**. This leads through paddy

fields to the **Henerathgoda Botanical Gardens** (daily 8am–6pm; charge) at Asgiriya. Established in 1876, this pretty park contains 400 species of plants in 14.4 hectares (36 acres). You'll probably have the gardens to yourself as they are little visited by tourists.

WARAKAPOLA

Return to the Kandy Road. After the village of Pasyala is the hamlet of **Cadjugama** ❶, where women in brightly coloured blouses offer cashew nuts (cadju) to passing motorists from roadside stalls. Stop to taste the nuts, either plain, salted or with chilli, at Dimuthukaju, 51 Kandy Road, Bataleeya, Pasyala (daily 6.30am–10.30pm), which also has toilet facilities.

Next, the road runs a gauntlet of village houses and stalls at **Warakapola** ❷, where craftsmen skilfully weave cane into chairs, baskets and odd souvenirs. At **Ambepussa**, 60km (37 miles) from Colombo, is the country's oldest existing hostelry, see ⑪①, opened in 1828 when the road was being built.

There the A6 branches off the A1, heading northwards via **Kurunegala** to Dambulla and Trincomalee.

PINNAWELA ELEPHANT ORPHANAGE

Continue on the A1, where heavier traffic 79km (49 miles) from Colombo indicates bustling **Kegalle**. A good spot for lunch and a drink is **Salika Inn**, see ⑪②; then leave the main

Above from far left: inside the ornate Shrine of the Tooth in Kandy; Pinnawela Elephant Orphanage.

Food and Drink ⑪

① AMBEPUSSA REST HOUSE
Ambepussa; tel: 035-226 7299; daily 12.30–4pm, 7.30–10pm; $$
Marking the halfway point between Colombo and Kandy, this rest house is very popular with local travellers for rice and curry lunches or sandwiches in a tranquil atmosphere. It also has a shop packed with craft souvenirs.

② SALIKA INN
118 Colombo Road, Kegalle; tel: 035-222 2876; daily 6am–10pm; $$
With a formal upstairs restaurant and a less formal bar-restaurant on its mezzanine, Salika Inn caters for Kegalle's lawyers and other professionals with low-priced spicy curries or fish dishes and quick service.

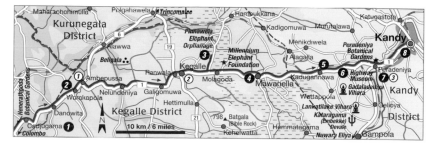
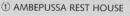

Above from left: deep in prayer at the Temple of the Tooth; a moat encircles the Temple; a friendly tussle at Pinnawela.

Above: clay pots and jars are big business in Molagoda.

road to head northwards to Pinnawela. The state-run **Pinnawela Elephant Orphanage ❸** (daily 8.30am–6pm; charge) is about a 5km (3-mile) drive past some small, privately operated elephant sideshows. Don't stop, but go for the real thing. There are more than 80 elephants in the orphanage, from calves of only a few weeks to magnificent, fully mature animals.

Try to visit the orphanage during feeding times at 9.15am, 1.15pm and 5pm, or during bathing times, 10am–noon and 2–4pm. Bathing takes place at the end of the road opposite the entrance to the orphanage compound. Buy your tickets at the main entrance and walk down the road to the river, taking a seat at one of several restaurants for refreshment while watching the elephants lumbering in the water.

BIBLE ROCK

Returning to the Kandy Road, you will see hundreds of clay pots and jars on display on both sides of the road at **Molagoda**. A solitary hill, **Utu-**

wankanda, indicates the place where Saradiel, Sri Lanka's Robin Hood, lived in the 19th century.

At **Mawanella ❹**, look up to see fruit bats hanging from trees along the banks of the Maha Oya (river). As the road climbs, the scenery becomes breathtaking, with terraced paddy fields, lush green vegetation and sheer drops down the cliff side. **Bible Rock** (Batgala), so named because it resembles an open Bible, comes into view on the right. Beside the road, stalls sell avocado pears and the pungent-smelling durian.

KADUGANNAWA AND THE HIGHWAY MUSEUM

There is a slender obelisk, 38m (125ft) in height, on a bluff on the southern side of the road at **Kadugannawa ❺**. This commemorates Captain W.F. Dawson (died 1829), 'whose science and skill planned and executed this road and other works of public utility', according to a plaque. The road was built in 1820, the tower erected in 1832. A further tribute to road-making skills is the unusual **Highway Museum ❻** (Sat–Thur 8am–5pm, free), opened in 1986, with its display of steamrollers and antique road-making equipment.

Tea Museum
The formidable granite building on the southern side of the Kandy Road at Peradeniya, 107km (67 miles) from Colombo) is the newly built **Tea Fort-**

ress, see ⑪③, where connoisseur-class teas can be sampled and purchased. On the southern side of the road where it curves down into **Peradeniya** ❼, there is a private museum of classic cars dating from the 1920s, but it is open only occasionally.

KANDY

Kandy ❽, nestling among green hills with a lake as its centrepiece, is the best laid out of all Sri Lanka's cities. It was the seat of the last king of Sri Lanka until the British captured him in 1815.

Temple of the Tooth

To get an impression of the city before exploring it, drive first around the lake up **Rajapihilla Mawatha** to the viewpoint at the top, where you can appreciate the full glory of Kandy below. To the right, the **Temple of the Tooth** ❶ (Sri Dalada Maligawa; daily 5.30am– 8.30pm; charge), complete with a golden roof, looks resplendent. Return to the main street, Dalada Veediya (Lake Drive), to visit the octagonal temple, where the tooth of the Buddha, brought to Sri Lanka in the 4th century from India, is enshrined. The tooth is Sri Lanka's most venerated object, and a replica is paraded through the streets during the **Esala Perahera** procession, held for 10 days in July or August

Walk through a small fenced park to reach the temple. The tooth itself can only be seen by the most important of

visitors, but its ornately decorated shrine and the reverent atmosphere pervading the inner temple are memorable. The tall wooden pillars are typical of Kandyan architecture.

To the north is a museum with the remains of a magnificent tusker, Raja, who carried the temple's treasure in the Esala Perahera for many years.

*Kandyan Arts &
Crafts Association*

The colonial **Queen's Hotel**, back down Dalada Veediya to the west, is a convenient place to stay or have an

Dress Code

There are security checks at each of the three entrances to the fenced park in front of the temple. A notice requests visitors to refrain from wearing 'headdresses, miniskirts, short trousers, sleeveless jackets and to help maintain the sanctity of the area'. Footwear must be left at a stall in front of the temple.

Peradeniya Gardens

About 6.5km (4 miles) southwest of Kandy, the Peradeniya Botanical Gardens (daily 7.30am–5.45pm; charge) are the island's largest and finest. Enclosed in a loop of the Mahaweli Ganga (river), the lush 60-hectare (147-acre) park, originally part of the royal residence of King Kirti Sri Rajasinha (1747–80), became a botanical garden in 1821. The first tea seedlings were planted here in 1824, nearly 50 years before tea proved its worth as a commercially profitable crop.

The gardens offer a bewildering array of tropical trees and plants plus a charming orchid house, and merit at least a couple of hours' exploring, either on foot or in a hired bullock cart. At 550m (1,804ft) above sea level, the gardens have an average daytime temperature of 26°C (79°F) – it is best to visit before 10am or after 4pm, when they are at their most pleasant.

Above from left:
scenic Kandy Lake;
traditional Kandyan
dancing and
drumming; tuk-tuks
awaiting fares.

evening drink in its **Pub Royale**, see
🍴④. Or opt for the kitsch and eccen-
tricity of **Helga's Folly** to make your
night in Kandy especially memorable;
more modest with astonishing views of
the lake is the **Salika Inn**. Both are set
high on the hillside south of the lake.

Take the chance offered by a night in
Kandy to see a traditional dancing show.
At the **Kandyan Arts & Crafts Association B** in Avanhala (near the
Temple of the Tooth), an hour-long
performance of traditional dancing and
drumming begins at 6pm every evening.
Your hotel desk can arrange tickets, for
which there is a charge.

Kandy Lake
The next day, take a lakeside stroll. It
is no longer possible to drive around
the entire lake, but from the Queen's

Hotel you can walk along the pavement between the temple park fence
and the lake. The building on the lake's
embankment, now a police barracks,
was once the **Royal Bathhouse**.

British Garrison Cemetery
When you reach the end of the security fence surrounding the temple,
cross the road and walk up the steps
opposite. About 100m/yds up the
sloping road, you come to a small
granite-block lodge at the entrance to
the **Garrison Cemetery C** (7/11
Angarika Dharmapala Mawatha; daily
8am–1pm, 2–5pm; donation). Here in
a neatly kept setting, not far from the
Udawattekelle Sanctuary, are the
graves of early British settlers, including
Sir John D'Oyly (1774–1824), the first
Resident of the Kandy Provinces. His

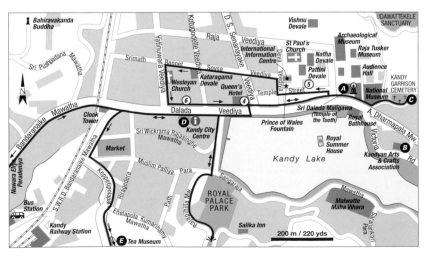

headstone recalls his services to Britain from his arrival in 1802, for which he was made a baronet.

Prince of Wales Fountain

It's a long hike around the lake (built in 1810–12), so you might prefer to return in the direction of the Queen's Hotel, then pass in front of the temple and around the other side along Temple Street. The **Olde Empire Hotel**, see ⑪⑤, is good for rice and curry.

Turn northwards past an open-sided Kandyan pavilion to enter the street called Deva Veediya, opposite an Edwardian-era block of lawyers' offices. There you'll be astonished to see an unlikely (and rarely spouting) **fountain** of chubby cherubs. Built in Glasgow, it was erected by planters to commemorate a visit to Kandy by the Prince of Wales in 1875.

Shopping District

The fountain is within a few minutes' walk of the **International Information Centre** (daily 8am–4pm), where books on Kandy can be purchased. The road continues to **St Paul's Church**, but it is blocked by a security barrier, so take the road westwards (Srimath Bennet Soysa Veediya) to enter the shopping district. Turn southwards down Yatinuwara Veediya to return to Dalada Veediya, where there is an office of the Sri Lanka **Tourism Promotion Bureau** (tel: 081-222 2661; daily 8.30am–5pm) in the new glass-fronted mall, **Kandy City**

Centre ⑪, next to the Cargills Food City complex and opposite **The Pub**, see ⑪⑥. You'll also find dress shops, bakeries and hardware stores.

Tea Museum

Before you leave Kandy, drive in the direction of the railway station and turn southwards at the clock tower to enter a road to the east, signposted to the **Tea Museum ⑤** (Hantana; daily 8.15am–4.30pm; charge). Housed in an old tea factory are exhibits tracing the story of tea and the pioneers who produced it, including James Taylor (1835–92), who began the first tea plantation at Loolecondra, south of Kandy, in 1868.

Food and Drink 🍴

④ PUB ROYALE
4 Dalada Veediya; tel: 081-223 3026; daily 11am–11pm; $
At a corner of the Queen's Hotel, this pub seems not to have changed since colonial days; good for hearty drinking and snacks like fish buns and deep-fried rolls stuffed with vegetables from the associated pastry counter.

⑤ OLDE EMPIRE HOTEL
21 Temple Street; tel: 081-222 4284; daily 11.30am–3.30pm, 6–9.30pm; $
Famous on the travellers' grapevine for its budget accommodation, this old hotel has a ground-floor restaurant that serves some of the best rice and curry in Sri Lanka, tasting as though slow-cooked in a clay pot on a wood fire.

⑥ THE PUB
36 Dalada Veediya; tel: 081-223 4341; daily 11am–11pm (bar closed 2–5pm); $$
Above a bakery, you can join locals and tourists sitting on the balcony to watch activity in the main street below, or dine inside on Western fare with chips and boiled vegetables in the dimly lit restaurant.

HILL COUNTRY

This tour, through tea-clad hillsides to the former colonial retreat of Nuwara Eliya, gives an enchanting glimpse of the hill country where the temperature can drop to 10°C (50°F), although it's within seven degrees of the Equator.

DISTANCE 248km (154 miles)

TIME Two days

START Kandy

END Colombo

POINTS TO NOTE

It is possible to make this trip by train from Kandy (or from Colombo) to Nanu Oya station, the closest station to Nuwara Eliya. Licensed freelance guides, such as the highly recommended Selvam (tel: 077-632 6663), wait at the station to help tourists.

Instead of returning to Colombo the next day, you could embark on tour 8 to Haputale.

Food and Drink 🍴

① PUSSELAWA REST HOUSE

Pusselawa; tel: 081-247 8397; www.ceylonhotels.lk; daily 12.30–3pm, 7–9pm; $

Open throughout the day for refreshments, this small, basic rest house of only three rooms is poised over a magnificent valley view. It is reliable for lunchtime rice and curry served in its glass-walled restaurant extension.

Nuwara Eliya is a haunting reminder of British rule, because of its setting and colonial-style houses. In 1828, the governor, Sir Edward Barnes (1776–1838), promoted the highland site as a health retreat for British officials who wanted to escape the oppressive heat of the lowlands.

The bungalow that was originally built for Barnes expanded to become in 1891 the mock-Tudor Grand Hotel, setting the style for other mansions, turning Nuwara Eliya (it means 'royal city of light') into a tropical version of a UK county town. Fashionable circles in Colombo converge here in April, when temperatures begin to rise in the commercial capital. The green hills, the cool weather, the beautiful lake and parks, make Nuwara Eliya the most pleasant and popular hill resort on the island.

GAMPOLA

On leaving Kandy at the beginning of the morning's drive to Nuwara Eliya, the A1 road leads past the **Peradeniya Botanical Gardens** *(see p.49)*, so there is an opportunity to drop in there. Afterwards, take the branch off the A1 to pick up the A5 signposted to Gam-

pola. Another way is to follow the road due south out of Kandy until the second roundabout and take the road from there, signposted to Galaha, as this leads through the picturesque campus of the **Peradeniya University**. About 3.5km (2 miles) further there is a 'Y' junction with the right fork leading along the old road to Gampola. A hosted plantation bungalow near here, called **Ellerton**, is one of many in the area that welcomes guests for the night.

In spite of having been a 14th-century capital, the main interest of **Gampola** ❶, 20km (12½ miles) south of Kandy, is as a busy town at the gateway to the tea districts of the hill country. There is a cottage **rest house**, see 🍴①, in the village of **Pusselawa**, some 20km (12 miles) further along the well-made A5 highway. Another former tea planter's bungalow accommodating guests in renovated colonial luxury, **Lavender House**, is located here.

Above from far left: an early-morning view over hill country from the Heritance Tea Factory Hotel; Tamil tea-pickers at work in the plantations.

Above: a hill-country tea factory; young monks make their way to class.

English Vegetables

English vegetables were introduced to Sri Lanka by Samuel Baker (1821–93), the explorer famous for discovering the source of the Nile, when he started an English-style settlement in Nuwara Eliya in the 1840s.

RAMBODA FALLS

About 10km (6 miles) past Pusselawa, the road skirts the magnificent **Ramboda Falls ❷**, which tumble over the cliffs in two 100m (328ft) high cascades. As the road twists and turns uphill, boys clutching bunches of flowers run up the hillsides to offer flowers for sale where vehicles slow down at the narrow bends.

Some 15km (9 miles) before Nuwara Eliya, the **Labookellie Tea Factory**, see ⓉⒺ② (www.mackwoodstea.com; daily 8.30am–6.30pm; donation), hosts guided tours explaining how tea is made, as well as letting visitors walk

through the tea gardens, and drink tea in its garden café or buy tea to take away in packets. The factory is at 1,500m (4,921ft) above sea level, so you may begin to notice a drop in temperature.

NUWARA ELIYA

The road swings into **Nuwara Eliya ❸** past the aptly named **St Andrew's Hotel** beside the bright green links of the 36-hectare (90-acre) **Nuwara Eliya Golf Club Ⓐ** (tel: 052-222 2835; daily 8am–7pm; charge), established in 1889. The 18-hole course is one of the best, and lushest, in the entire continent, although it is criss-crossed by the town's roads and footpaths. Visitors are welcome to play or to look around. Buried behind the clubhouse is the body of Major Thomas William Rogers, a doughty empire-builder reputed to have killed 1,300 elephants. He died in 1845 when he was struck by lightning while sheltering at a rest house near Nuwara Eliya. His grave shows a repaired crack and is said to have itself been struck by lightning.

Drive slowly through the town to take in the sights. Before the crossroads as you approach the northern end of the main street, on the left, at Number 20, is a Nuwara Eliya institution, **The Lion Pub**, see ⓉⒺ③. With crumbling entrance steps and packed with friendly vegetable farmers in woolly caps and cotton sarongs, it is a real slice of hill-country life.

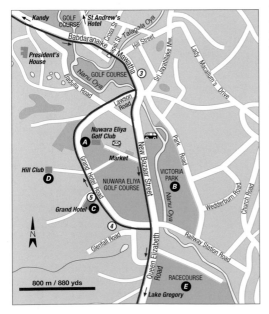

Market Place

Turn into New Bazaar Street, the town's main street, for the short drive past the covered **market place** (daily 6am–6pm), where hill country fruit and vegetables, like strawberries, miniature potatoes, bright cauliflowers and plump leeks, sell for much less than they do in Colombo. Opposite is an open-air courtyard with stalls where you can buy woollen sweaters, hats and jackets, to keep warm in the surprising chill that grips Nuwara Eliya at night. People walk fast or jog here, not because they are in a hurry but to keep warm.

Victoria Park

The pink brick spire ahead marks the colonial-built **post office**, while opposite is **Victoria Park B**, opened in 1897 and best visited during the April season when it is bright with blooms for the annual best garden competition. This is usually won by the **Grand Hotel C**, whose gardens are carefully tended in keeping with its image as a stately English mansion. The Grand Hotel road to the east leads past the **King Prawn**, see ⑪④, specialising in spicy Chinese dishes, while at the hotel gates is the **Grand Indian**, see ⑪⑤, for fast food or takeaways.

Racecourse and Lake

The road curves past the Grand Hotel with the golf course on the right to reach the **Hill Club D**, a hoary granite hotel steadfastly withstanding modern trends, with gentlemen required to wear jackets and ties (supplied if required) for dinner. Its interior, complete with stags' heads and time-worn books, is a perfect period piece. The service of tea in the lounge here with shuffling waiters wearing white gloves is a ritual.

Food and Drink

② LABOOKELLIE TEA CENTRE

Labookellie Eatste; tel: 052-223 5806; www.mackwoodstea.com; daily 8.00am–6.30pm; $

After a tour of the factory, visitors stop for a cup of single-estate tea (that is tea that's not been blended with tea from other estates) and slabs of chocolate cake in a congenial atmosphere in the factory's tea café and garden. This is a sister tea outlet to the Tea Breeze in Colombo (see tour 2).

③ THE LION PUB

20 Kandy Road (Old Bazaar Street/Bandaranaike Mawatha), Nuwara Eliya; daily 11am–10pm; $

Serves draught and bottled beer to preserve the popularity of the original beer brewed in Nuwara Eliya. Waiters deliver the beer in mugs, jugs and mini glass barrels to a carousing crowd. Plenty of snacks, including succulent fried local beef.

④ KING PRAWN

Glendower Hotel, 5 Grand Hotel Road, Nuwara Eliya; tel: 052-222 2501; daily noon–3.30pm, 7–10pm; $$$

Set in the cosy dining room of the Glendower bungalow hotel, with wooden slabs as tables and a log fire at night, the King Prawn specialises in fiery Chinese cuisine to keep the cold at bay.

⑤ GRAND INDIAN

Grand Hotel, Grand Hotel Road, Nuwara Eliya; tel: 052-222 2881; www.tangerinehotels.com; daily noon–3pm, 6–9.30pm; $$

Indian dishes served in a fast-food atmosphere at the gates of the Grand Hotel; good for a quick meal or a takeaway without the formality of eating in the hotel's restaurants.

Residents at Rest
Many of the pioneers who created Nuwara Eliya are buried in the Anglican Holy Trinity Church behind Victoria Park. The church was built in 1853 but has been considerably enlarged over the years. Many settlers died being thrown from their horses, or from roofs or rocks falling on them. Among those buried here is Arthur Sydney Reeves (1848–91), murdered by his servant while having dinner.

Return to the main road for a drive past the **racecourse ⓔ**, where race meets attracting Colombo's fashionable set are held in April and August, and **Lake Gregory**, where boating is sometimes possible. Standing on the shores of the lake, you should be able to see (unless it's too misty) **Mount Pidurutalagala**, at 2,524m (8,281ft) the highest mountain in Sri Lanka, towering 635m (2,081ft) above the town.

KANDAPOLA

Although many visitors stay at a colonial guesthouse or hotel in the town, there is a chance to relax in the tea-growing hills at the **Heritance Tea Factory Hotel**. Take the road eastwards from the Grand Hotel junction to the plantation town of **Kandapola ❹**. A signposted track leads northwards uphill through vegetable and tea gardens to reach the hotel at 2,200m (7,214ft) above sea level. Converted from an abandoned tea factory retaining the exterior walls and casement windows, it has a luxurious interior created in lofts once used for tea-drying.

Nature Treks

Even if you are not staying here it is worth a visit to marvel at the interior with furniture fashioned out of old machinery or to have dinner in its converted **Railway Carriage Restaurant TCK 6685**, see ⑪⑥. A highlight are the two-hour nature treks that take place three times a day, at 6.30am, 10am and 4pm (charge). These guided jungle walks cover 7km (4 miles), taking in the hotel's rose, organic vegetable and tea gardens. Guests learn about the tea plucking and manufacturing process and can pick the leaves to receive – the next morning – a packet of the manufactured tea they have plucked themselves. The trek leads past the Hethersett village kovil and into the nearby Kuduratte Jungle, a carefully conserved forest that is home to amazing numbers of birds, butterflies and mammals.

HAKGALA BOTANICAL GARDENS

The next day, after a hearty breakfast at your hotel, there's time for exploring before heading back to Colombo or deeper into tea country *(see tour 8, p.58)*. At 10km (6 miles) south of Nuwara Eliya is the prominent peak, **Hakgala Rock**, whose sheer face rises 450m (1,500ft) above the surrounding countryside. At the foot of the rock lie the delightful **Hakgala Botanical Gardens ❺** (daily 8am–5pm; charge). With an area of 24 hectares (59 acres) at 1,884m (6,182 ft) above sea level, this was begun in 1860 as an experimental plantation of cinchona trees, from which quinine is derived. With a herbarium, a rose garden, a fernery and a wild-orchid collection, the gardens attract more than 400,000 visitors a year, mostly schoolchildren.

HORTON PLAINS NATIONAL PARK

Beyond Hakgala, at the southern edge of the hill country and 32km (20 miles) from Nuwara Eliya, lies **Horton Plains National Park ❻** (daily 6am–6.30pm, ticket office closes at 4pm; charge). While it is home to wildlife like sambhur (large deer), the scenery often shrouded in mist – is the attraction. The park offers excellent hikes, the most popular being the 9km (5½-mile) round trip from the entrance to **World's End** (Kirgalpotta), a stunning viewpoint at the very edge of the hill country, where the cliffs fall away for the best part of 1,000m (3,288ft) to the plains below.

BACK TO COLOMBO

Returning to the park entrance, you could continue on the A5 to Ella *(see tour 8, p.63)* or return to Nuwara Eliya. If you are driving back to Colombo, take the A7 signposted to Hatton through **Nanu Oya** (or go to Nanu Oya to catch the train). Off the A7 take the northern fork diverting to **Radella ❼**, where the Somerset Estate has a shop (daily 8am–6pm) selling packets of estate-grown tea, strawberries and home-made strawberry jam.

Back on the A7 bound for Colombo, drive through **Talawakele ❽** and glorious tea country, keeping an eye open for two waterfalls, St Clair and Devon on the northern valley side of the road.

There are roadside viewpoints, while a commanding view of the whole valley is to be had from the battlements of the **Tea Castle**, see ⑪⑦, an extraordinary new building with a restaurant and tea shop. From there it's a 50km (31-mile) drive to **Kitulgala ❾**, with its delightful, if laidback, **rest house**, see ⑪⑧, for lunch or dinner overlooking the river made famous as the location for the film *The Bridge on the River Kwai*. It's another 86km (53 miles) via Avissawella back to Colombo.

Food and Drink

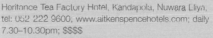

⑥ RAILWAY CARRIAGE RESTAURANT TCK 6685
Heritance Tea Factory Hotel, Kandapola, Nuwara Eliya; tel: 052 222 9600; www.aitkenspencehotels.com; daily 7.30–10.30pm; $$$$
This unique restaurant, open to non-resident guests too, is named after the restored narrow-gauge railway carriage in which it is located, adjoining the Heritance Tea Factory Hotel restaurant. The superb seven-course set menu includes lots of choice, like locally farmed venison in rosemary gravy.

⑦ TEA CASTLE
Talawakele; tel: 051-222 2561; www.mlesnateas.com; daily 8am–6pm; $$
From the outside it looks like a miniature castle, but inside it is a charming restaurant for authentic rice and curry from a menu, or for a top-quality cup of tea and scrumptious cake.

⑧ KITULGALA REST HOUSE
Kitulgala; tel: 036-567 2333; www.ceylonhotels.lk; daily breakfast 7–10am, lunch 12.30–4.30pm, dinner 7.30–10pm; $$
Convenient for a quick meal from the rice-and-curry buffet set out in a large restaurant (with a bar) overlooking the Kitulgala river, or if you have time to wait while it's freshly prepared, try the Club Sandwich with a layers of ham, egg, cheese and chicken mayonnaise.

8

HAPUTALE, ELLA AND BANDARAWELA

This tour takes you through real tea country, where the high-grown tea, nurtured by sun-drenched days and chilly, dewy nights, covers the hills and dales, and plantation bungalows commanding superb views offer homely accommodation and traditional planter's fare.

Plantation Life

British planters always chose the best locations for their bungalows, so they could keep an eye on the labourers in the tea fields below, and enjoy panoramic views. To stay in one of these, waited upon by butler and cook and dining on traditional fare like mulligatawny soup, fish pie and trifle, is to taste the colonial planter's lifestyle.

DISTANCE 70km (43 miles)
TIME One or two days
START Nuwara Eliya
END Ella Gap
POINTS TO NOTE
This journey can also be made by rail from Nanu Oya station (near Nuwara Eliya) for a two-hour scenic train ride along hilltop ridges. It soars above fertile valleys and dives down long tunnels, via the island's highest station, Pattipola, 1,891m (6,203ft) above sea level, to Haputale. From Ella you can drive south for 134km (83 miles) to visit Yala National Park (tour 12).

Few are the tourists and tour buses you'll encounter on this route, a leisurely sampling of the countryside where forests have given way to thousands of acres of tea, and local culture has a Hindu rather than a Buddhist influence. The hills are alive with tea- pluckers, and everyone seems to be going about their daily business, either working in tea production and vegetable allotments or crowding into small village shops to buy provisions.

NUWARA ELIYA TO HAPUTALE

The drive from Nuwara Eliya along the A5 allows an opportunity to visit the **Hakgala Botanical Gardens** *(see tour 7)*. After a further 15km (9-mile) drive through hills, forest and tea, take the road turning south at the small town of **Keppetipola**. This eventually wends its way around many bends to Haputale. If you have time, stop at **Idalgashina** ❶ and visit its railway station, at 1,615m (5,298ft) above sea level, for its stunning views of a lunar-like landscape and scalloped hills dropping away from both sides of the platform. The tea gardens here are organic (no artificial fertiliser is used to promote growth) and produce special long-leaf premium tea as well as unique Sri Lankan green tea.

Adisham

About 3km (2 miles) before Haputale the country lane brings you to **Adisham ❷** (tel: 057-226 8030; *Poya* days and school holidays only 9.30am–12.30pm and 1.30–4pm; charge). Now used as a monastery and novitiate by the Congregation of St Sylvester, a missionary order that came to the country in 1840, this Gothic, granite-block house was originally built in 1931 as the home of Sir Thomas Villiers (1869–1959). His grandfather, Lord John Russell, was twice prime minister of Britain, but Villiers was the black sheep of the family and arrived in Ceylon in 1887 with ten pounds in his pocket.

He prospered and rewarded himself for his successful business dealings by building Adisham as an expression of his nostalgia – he modelled it on Leeds Castle in Kent, and named it Adisham after the rectory where he was born. He furnished it with imported carpets, porcelain, furniture and glassware, and Villiers's fine library remains as he left it. The house is only open on public and school holidays, but it is worth a visit to see this strange, chilling monument to the 1930s on a hill in the tropics.

HAPUTALE

The attraction of **Haputale ❸** is hard to define: most visitors just gasp at the sight of the main street which seems to tumble off the edge of a cliff, and hurry on to the more cosmopolitan town of Bandarawela. But Haputale, in spite of its grubby streets contrasting with the

Above from far left: inside time-warped Adisham; Haputale tea plantations.

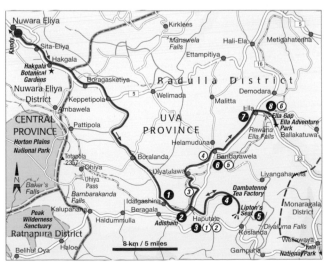

Nature Reserve
Even if Adisham isn't open, the Tangamalai Nature Reserve (daily 8am–5pm; charge) directly beyond it is worth visiting. A beautiful area of tropical forest, it is home to a rich array of bird life, with lots of monkeys too.

On a bluff above Haputale town centre and its bus station, the small 19th-century St Andrew's Church, administered by the Interdenominational Church in Colombo but looking as if it has been transported from British shires, is fascinating for its gravestone inscriptions of 19th- and 20th-century British residents.

carefully tended tea plantations around it, has an agreeable quality. Perhaps it is its compact size and sense of activity; its climate that changes from warm sunshine to freezing mist in seconds; or its eccentricities, like the railway track running through the town (which also serves as a market place for vendors, who have to move their wares quickly whenever a train comes along).

Lunch Options

You can walk around this charming, friendly town in 10 minutes and see where the main road skirts the long drop down to the plains below. There is an efficient communications centre, **Website Link Cyber Café** (3 UC Complex, Station Road; tel: 057-226

8613; daily 8am–7pm), where you can stop for a pot of tea by the tiny garden beside the railway line. Train times are posted there, and the proprietor, Loga, is happy to act as a guide for trekkers or for visitors to Lipton's Seat.

For lunch there is the **Erechtheum Restaurant**, see ⑪①, in a modern hotel (Olympus Plaza) designed for tourists on the outskirts of town; or pop into a famous local drinking den, **High Cliffe**, see ⑪②, by the rail track.

Plantation Bungalows

However, the reason for visiting Haputale is to stay in one of the extraordinary plantation bungalows close to the town. When you take the road eastwards to Lipton's Seat, you

Right: pretty flowers and breathtaking scenery at Kelburne Mountain Resort.

pass above three of these, tucked into the hillside with views across the plains right down to the south coast.

The four-bedroom **Sherwood Bungalow** (reservations tel: 011-238 1644; www.forthotels.lk) has an old-fashioned air to it, with a garden gazebo instead of a veranda for nature-watching while having a cup of estate tea.

A little further from the town, **Kelburne Mountain Resort** (tel: 057-226 8029; www.kelburncmountainview.com) has three separate bungalows grouped around a central plateau where meals are served in a pavilion, or to the dining rooms of each bungalow.

The grandest, 3km (2 miles) from Haputale, is **Thotalagala** (reservations tel: 011-238 1644; www.forthotels.lk), set in a garden of ponds and flowers and with a secluded swimming pool for the hardy. It consists of three linked pavilions with a teak-panelled smoking room and log fire.

Dambatenne Tea Factory

Although it's only 13km (8 miles) from Haputale to Lipton's Seat, the drive takes time because the road is too narrow in places for vehicles to pass each other, and much of it is unsurfaced. The road passes alongside the **Dambatenne Tea Factory** ❹, at 105m (345ft) the longest in the island. Dambatenne was one of many estates owned by Sir Thomas Lipton (1848–1931), the Scottish grocer who was hugely successful in marketing tea worldwide.

Lipton's Seat

When Lipton stayed on the island he would ride his horse up to the estate's highest point, now called **Lipton's Seat** ❺ (daily 7.30am–6pm; charge) to survey his tea gardens. There is a sign and a lookout pavilion there now. Though always beautiful, the morning is a particularly good time to go, before clouds obscure the view.

Breakfast

If you stay the night in one of the plantation bungalows on the road back to Haputale, the next morning your butler will wake you with 'bed tea' before a hearty breakfast of eggs and bacon or beef curry and egg hoppers (crisp pancakes with a fried egg in the centre).

Food and Drink

① ERECHTHEUM RESTAURANT
Olympus Plaza Hotel, 75 Welimada Road, Haputale; tel: 057-226 8544; www.olympusplazahotel.com; daily 7.30am–9.30pm; $$
In a glass-walled hotel with 26 rooms and a rooftop bar with a view, this ground-floor restaurant serves à la carte meals of Western dishes like pork chops, or rice and chicken curry on demand.

② HIGH CLIFFE
15 Station Road, Haputale; tel: 057-226 8096; daily 9am–10pm, $
This bar, whose entrance is hidden behind a brick wall, has evolved over the years from a tiny guesthouse with bunk beds for backpackers, to a neat 11-room hotel and bar-restaurant where snacks like beef with deep-fried garlic bulbs are sensational. You can sit with locals at tables with bells to summon stewards, or have your snacks in the private lounge upstairs.

Diyatalawa

Commence the drive to Ella by taking the A16 out of Haputale bound for Bandarawela but divert westwards after the hillside **New Rest House**, see ⑪③, to **Diyatalawa**. The road winds through a forest of eucalyptus pine trees down to a valley cantonment, a prison for Boers and then for German combatants in World War I and a convalescent camp for military personnel in World War II. The area has a salubrious, dry climate in contrast to the chill of Haputale. After passing through the town the road climbs up to join the A16 again.

BANDARAWELA

On a bend outside Bandarawela, an unprepossessing building called the **Riverside Inn**, see ⑪④, actually has a charming bar-restaurant in the garden behind it. The road swings into **Bandarawela ❻** alongside the railway track. Not as popular with foreign visitors as Nuwara Eliya, the town nevertheless boasts the **Bandarawela Hotel**, see ⑪⑤, built in 1893 when the railway arrived (Bandarawela was the terminus of the main line until the railway was extended to Badulla in 1924). With its tea-planter club atmosphere – a long lounge with chintzy armchairs and rooms with old-fashioned, brass-knobbed beds – it seems settled in the 1950s. Tea on the lawn served by tunic-and-sarong-wearing stewards is almost obligatory.

The beautiful hills around town are still the best area for what tea planters call 'flavoury tea'; pears and strawberries also reach their prime here, as the climate is drier and milder than at Nuwara Eliya.

From Leaf to Cup

Following the experimental growth of tea by James Taylor at Loolecondra near Kandy *(see tour 6)* in the 1860s, the topography of highland Sri Lanka was changed for ever. Large tracts of the hill country were cleared by British settlers attracted by the riches to be made from growing tea in a British colony. Within 20 years, the environment of the hill country was transformed from dense jungle to swathes of neatly manicured tea bushes. In time, the best area to grow flavourful tea was discovered to be around Bandarawela.

Tea begins its journey from hillside to cup when two top leaves and a bud are gently picked by a tea plucker, usually female. The freshly gathered leaves are swiftly transferred to a nearby tea factory where they are withered overnight in blasts of hot air to remove excess moisture. The withered leaves are rolled and crushed by machinery, often dating from Victorian times, to release the remaining sap and to trigger fermentation. The leaves are then fired in enormous ovens before being sifted and graded according to particle size. Orange Pekoe (OP) is the standard size for light tea without milk, while Broken Orange Pekoe Fannings (BOPF) is a small-size grade for a strong cup of tea mixed with milk and sugar.

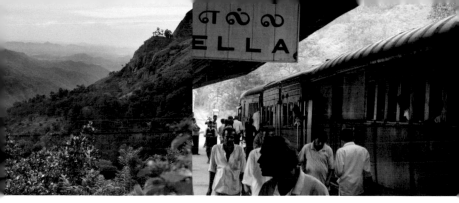

Dowa Cave Temple

Just 6km (4 miles) northeast of Bandarawela, the small **Dowa Cave Temple** stands right by the roadside, but is easily missed thanks to the thick woodland surrounding it. The main attraction here is a striking figure carved in bas-relief into the rock above the temple: either the historical Buddha or the future Buddha Maitreya.

ELLA

Just 2km (1 mile) further on the A16, at the southeastern cusp of the hills by the turn southwards on to the A23, is **Ella ❼**. A sleepy village a decade ago, it recently awakened with lots of guesthouses and cafés to cater for visitors attracted by the gorgeous view through a narrow cleft in the hills, known as **Ella Gap ❽**. See it comfortably from the garden of the **Grand Ella Motel**, see ⑪⑥.

Ella is also famous as one of the Sri Lankan sites most closely associated with the *Ramayana*, and particularly with the villainous Ravana, who is thought to have imprisoned Sita in the Rawana Ella Cave, just south of the village.

Rawana Ella Falls

Continuing southwards, there is a chance to buy factory-fresh tea at the **Kinellan Tea Centre** (daily 8am–6pm) before stopping to gaze at the **Rawana Ella Falls**. A great cataract of water

tumbles over a cliff right next to the road. Unfortunately, the graffiti scrawled on the rocks and the persistence of vendors trying to sell pink quartz contrasts with the beauty of the place. Near the 16km (10-mile) post further on, the **Ella Adventure Park** features log cabins in the jungle for a more serene experience of Ella's charms *(see p.101)*.

Above from far left: a colonial throwback at Bandarawela Hotel; early morning light brings out the beauty of Ella Gap; a train waits at Ella station.

Food and Drink

③ NEW REST HOUSE
Bandarawela Road, Haputale; tel: 057-492 8888; daily 6am–11pm; $
This seven-room rest house has a panoramic view of the Diyatalawa Valley from garden benches. Fried rice with chicken as well as freshly cooked rice and curry (no buffets) are specialities.

④ RIVERSIDE INN
Haputale Road, Bandarawela; tel: 057-222 2448; daily 11am–11pm; $
Chicken *biriyani* is available, washed down with a selection of local *arracks*, in this pretty, open-sided bar-restaurant in the back garden of a grim-looking building on the outskirts of Bandarawela.

⑤ BANDARAWELA HOTEL
14 Welimada Road, Bandarawela; tel: 057-222 2501; www.aitkenspencehotels.com; daily 10.30am–5.30pm; $$
Although this colonial hotel serves tea in its long lounge all day, mid-morning or mid-afternoon tea on the front lawn – in the sunshine or in the shade of the magnificent trees – is a memorable experience visitors shouldn't miss.

⑥ GRAND ELLA MOTEL
Ella; tel: 057-567 0711; www.ceylonhotels.lk; daily 7am–11pm; $$
With tables in a pavilion in the garden right at the edge of Ella Gap, this reincarnation of a rest house (it now has 14 non-AC rooms with minibar and TV) offers typical rice-and-curry fare or simpler sandwiches for a meal with a spectacular view.

9

DAMBULLA, SIGIRIYA AND ANURADHAPURA

A two-day excursion into the past, driving from the southernmost point of the Cultural Triangle (Kandy) to the northernmost point (Anuradhapura) with climbs up to the cave temple of Dambulla and to the top of the Lion Rock of Sigiriya, and a chance to explore a tropical arboretum.

Discount Permit
It is cheaper to buy a permit to visit all the Cultural Triangle sites at Kandy, Anuradhapura, Sigiriya and Polonnaruwa than it is to pay for tickets individually to visit each one. The permit can be obtained at the first site visited. Entrance to the Dambulla Cave Temple, however, costs extra.

DISTANCE 250km (155 miles)
TIME Two days
START Kandy
END Dambulla
POINTS TO NOTE
While starting the tour at Kandy makes it easier to visit the northern sights on the same day, you could also start in Colombo and take the A6 to Dambulla, then pick up the tour from there. It leads to Polonnaruwa (tour 10) – or if you've seen enough ruins you could head back south through Kandy and into the hill country.

Sri Lanka's cultural triangle – stretching from medieval Kandy to the ancient kingdoms of Anuradhapura to the north and Polonnaruwa to the east – is a treasure trove of cave temples, ruins more than 2,500 years old, the natural phenomenon of Sigiriya towering into the sky, and arid scenery in striking contrast to the lushness of the hill country.

DAMBULLA

Depart from **Kandy** *(see p.49)* after breakfast and drive northwards through Katugastota to join the A9. Pass through **Matale** towards **Dambulla**, 72km (45 miles) from Kandy and 153km (93 miles) along the A6 from Colombo. Some 3km (2 miles) before Dambulla on the A9, a large car park marks the entrance to **Dambulla Rock and Cave Temples ❶** (daily 7am–7pm; charge), the most impressive of Sri Lanka's many cave temples, and fronted by the largest gold Buddha statue in the world.

King Valagambahu fled here in the 1st century BC, when invaders from India captured Anuradhapura; after regaining his capital, the king built a temple in the caves where he had hidden. Later King Nissankamalla of Polonnaruwa gilded the interior of the caves, which became known as Rangiri (Golden Rock) Dambulla.

The 107m (350ft) climb to the temple is worth the effort. The five caves sit side-by-side beneath a huge rocky overhang and are filled with a veritable

treasury of Buddhist art, including innumerable statues of the Buddha and other deities, plus the finest selection of murals on the island.

Lunch Options

If you're already hungry, the **Thilanka Resort**, see ⑪①, is set off the road close to the temple compound; or try the **Dambulla Rest House**, see ⑪②, for traditional rest-house fare.

ANURADHAPURA

It's 86km (53 miles) from here to Anuradhapura along the A9. There are checks by the military and many permanently closed roads because **Anuradhapura ②** is a garrison town. It was also Sri Lanka's first capital, founded by King Pandukhabaya in 380 BC until, nearly 1,400 years later, the capital moved eastwards to Polon-

Above from far left: Dambula Rock and Cave Temples; the temples house a treasure trove of Buddhist art.

Food and Drink ⑪

① THILANKA RESORT
Godawolyaya, Moragollawa, Dambulla; tel: 066-446 8001; www.thilankaresorts.lk; daily 7.30–10.30am, 12.30–2.30pm, 7.30–10.30pm; $$$
In the middle of a mango orchard, created in flat scrubland stretching for 1km (½ mile) towards a river, is this 12-room luxury hotel. A sign outside advertises 'Special Lunches' for visitors to the cave temple. These consist of rice and curry served in banana leaf packets for a picnic in the garden, in a setting so tranquil it could make you want to stay longer.

② DAMBULLA REST HOUSE
Dambulla; tel: 066-228 4799; www.ceylonhotels.lk; daily 12.30–3pm, 7–9pm; $
This small (four-room) rest house is well run and serves snacks, lunch or drinks to walk-in guests who can relax on the shaded veranda or feast more formally on rice and curry in the dining room.

naruwa. Anuradhapura's 113 kings (and four queens) oversaw a great flowering of the arts, producing magnificent palaces, intricate sculptures, ornate pleasure gardens and a sequence of vast stupas built to protect the most sacred relics of Buddhism. Perhaps the most impressive achievement was in irrigation, with reservoirs constructed to preserve the monsoon rains, and a system of sluices put in place to keep the rice paddies productive.

Grand Hotel

The former Tissawewa Rest House, now known by its early 20th-century name of **Grand Hotel**, see 🍴③, set in what was formerly part of the Royal Pleasure Gardens, is a good place to plan an exploration of the ruins over a rice-and-curry lunch. You could get directions from the receptionist as to which roads are open.

Isurumuniya

You could start by heading south past the **Tissa Wewa Tank**, ascribed to King Devanampiyatissa who, in the 3rd century BC, made it Anuradhapura's

chief source of water. The **Isurumuniya** Ⓐ rock temple, built in the 3rd century BC as part of a monastic complex called Issiramana, is on the right.

Here stands the famous 4th-century AD limestone carving of the Isurumuniya lovers, a man and a woman immortalised in song. The woman lifts a warning finger but the man carries on regardless. It is said the figures represent Saliya, son of King Dutugemunu (161–137 BC), and a low-caste maiden whom he loved.

Sacred Bo Tree

Now drive north to see the **Sri Maha Bodhi** Ⓑ, the Sacred Bo Tree (tel: 025-222 2367; daily 6am–noon, 2–9.30pm; charge), the oldest historically documented tree in the world. Because of security concerns, you will have to park in the designated area about 1km (½ mile) south and walk.

The tree grew from a sapling of the original bo tree of Bodhgaya in India, under which the Buddha gained enlightenment. It was brought to Sri Lanka by Sangamitta, the daughter of Emperor Ashoka, in the 3rd century BC. Encircled by a gold-plated railing, it stands amid other younger trees. Most of the island's bo trees have been nurtured from the Sri Maha Bodhi's seeds.

Buddhists consider watering the bo tree an act of devotion, so you might see pilgrims, pots of water in hand, helping to nourish the plant.

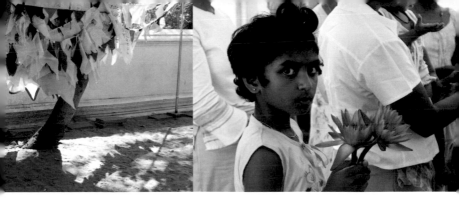

Brazen Palace

Within walking distance of the bo tree is the **Brazen Palace** **C** (Loha Pasada), which once had a bronze roof, nine floors and housed 1,000 monks. Only about 1,600 stone pillars now remain of its former splendours.

Anuradhapura Museum

You can drive to the **Anuradhapura Museum** **D** (tel: 025-222 2589; Sat–Wed 9am–5pm except public holidays; charge), which has numerous fine carvings from the Anuradhapura era and a model of the Thuparama Vatadage, complete with wooden roof. Among the interesting exhibits are the female figures on the guard stones, an indication that King Kassapa employed women as guards. There are agricultural tools, coins, pots and even impressions of a dog's paw and a man's toe on some bricks. Look out, too, for the museum's remarkable umbrella-like roof.

Above from far left: an ancient pool in Anuradhapura; prayer flags swathe a Bo tree; a young pilgrim brings floral offerings to Anuradhapura.

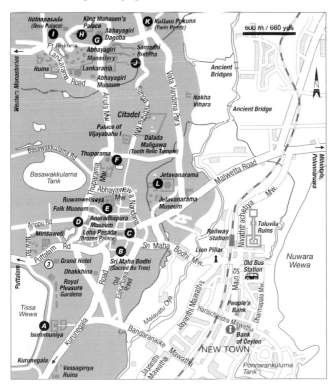

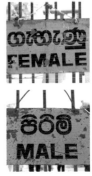

Above: his 'n' hers checkpoints in Anuradhapura.

Ruwanweliseya

Towards the north is the **Ruwanweliseya E**, a dagoba more than 150m (500ft) high, including a 90m (300ft) dome. The best-known construction by King Dutugemunu, it is regarded as probably the greatest of Anuradhapura's dagobas. The wall has a frieze of elephants, and the limestone statue is believed to represent Dutugemunu.

Thuparama

Continue driving to the north to the **Thuparama F**, which is not only the oldest dagoba on the island, but is believed to contain the right collarbone of the Buddha. The dagoba was built by King Devanampiyatissa and stands just over 20m (60ft) high. Constructed entirely out of earth in the 3rd century BC, this dagoba has

been embellished by a succession of rulers. Its present 'bell' shape is the result of major restoration work carried out in 1862.

Next take a drive along Anula Mawatha, towards the **Abhayagiri Dagoba G**, which was constructed by King Valagambahu (89–77 BC) and stands 74m (243ft) high. It is still undergoing restoration, with huge clumps of earth clinging to its base and bits of vegetation sprouting from its sides – a wonderfully romantic sight.

King Mahasen's Palace

By turning to **King Mahasen's Palace H**, among the ruins at the threshold of the Queen's Pavilion, you can observe the finest moonstone in Anuradhapura, cut on rock. To the west is the **Ratnapasada I**, built in the 8th century, and which has two of the best-preserved guard stones of the Anuradhapura era. The *naga* (snake) king sits under a *makara* (dragon) arch, with a flowerpot and lotus stalk – two symbols Sri Lankans associate with abundance and prosperity. Return to the Abhayagiri Dagoba, turn right at the crossroads and drive straight down to the **Samadhi Buddha J**, an excellent example of sculpture from the 4th century.

Kuttam Pokuna

Back at the crossroads, turn right and visit the beautiful **Kuttam Pokuna K** twin ponds, once a monks' bathing pool. Drive along the outer circular

---

Mihintale Shrines

According to legend, it was at Mihintale – literally Mahinda's Hill – that the Indian missionary Mahinda met and converted King Devanampiyatissa in 247 BC, establishing Buddhism as the island's religion.

Mihintale is unforgettable: a sequence of beautiful shrines, stupas and caves strung out across wooded hills and connected by broad flights of frangipani-shaded carved steps, usually clustered with crowds of devout, white-robed pilgrims. Its various shrines are connected by 1,840 steps, all of which must be climbed to reach the summit, where the Ambasthala Dagoba, or Mango Tree Stupa, supposedly marks the place where Mahinda surprised the king as he was hunting.

road (Vata Vandana) to the **Jeta-vanarama** ❻, Anuradhapura's largest dagoba. Built by King Mahasen (AD 273–303), it was originally over 122m (400ft) high, with a diameter of 110m (370ft). Occupying 3.2 hectares (8 acres) of land, it was just a little smaller than the Great Pyramid of Egypt.

HABARANA

Just 10km (6 miles) east of Anuradhapura along the A12 is **Mihintale** ❸, revered as the birthplace of Buddhism in Sri Lanka *(see feature)*. Afterwards, turn southwards along the A9 to drive 58km (36 miles) to **Habarana** ❹.

The **Habarana Rest House**, see ⑪④, is good for simple refreshment. At Habarana's junction of four main highways, take the southern A6 for the 10-minute drive to stay overnight at the **Cinnamon Lodge** with its **Ehala Restaurant**, see ⑪⑤, or in its charming neighbour **Chaaya Village**.

SIGIRIYA

After breakfast, to avoid the midday heat, leave as early as you can for the drive along country roads to **Sigiriya** ❺ (Lion Rock). The easiest way is to turn south at the hotels' exit onto the A6 and after about 26km (16 miles), turn left at the Sigiriya sign and continue along the unmade road which gives glimpses of the 200m (650ft) golden rock sprouting from the jungle.

Museum and Gardens

Sigiriya Palace (daily 7am–5pm; charge) was built on top of the huge rock as an impregnable fortress by King Kassapa (AD 447–95), who had killed his father and feared revenge from his brother.

There are licensed freelance guides available close to the entrance to the park surrounding the Sigiriya rock, who can explain the history in detail. There is also a **museum** (daily 8am–4.30pm; free) dedicated to the Sigiriya story, about a 300m/yd walk northwest after passing through the park entrance enclosure before the Sigiriya complex.

The only access is through the mouth of a lion statue carved halfway up the monolith. A moat filled with crocodiles once guarded the foot of the rock and water gardens were created around it; these are undergoing restoration.

Above from far left: elephants guard the Ruwanweliseya; murals and a Buddha in the Ruwanweliseya image house.

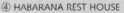

Food and Drink

④ HABARANA REST HOUSE

Habarana; tel: 066-227 0003; www.ceylonhotels.lk; daily 11.45am–3pm, 6–10pm; $
Another small (four-room) country rest house, in a central location close to the important Habarana junction of the A6 and A11 roads. Attracts custom for drinks on its veranda or in the garden, and rice and curry for lunch and dinner.

⑤ EHALA RESTAURANT

Cinnamon Lodge, Habarana; tel: 066-227 0011; www.cinnamonhotels.com; daily 12.30–2.30pm, 7.30–10pm; $$$
The Ehala Restaurant, by the swimming pool of the Cinnamon Lodge hotel, is open to non-residents and serves lavish international buffets. Special dining experiences, such as in a boat on the lake, in the jungle or a riverside barbecue, can be arranged.

Above from left:
baby elephant on the
approach to Sigiriya;
Habarana sunset.

Sigiriya Frescoes

A strenuous climb up a brick stairway and spiral staircase leads you to Sigiriya's single most celebrated sight, the so-called **Sigiriya Damsels**. Commissioned by Kassapa in the 5th century, it is an exquisite mural, perhaps the largest ever attempted, painted in brilliant colours onto the sheer rock face and featuring 21 beautiful, bare-chested women, swathed in cloud from the waist down.

No one knows whether the seductive beauties were meant to be goddesses, Kassapa's concubines or dancers. Impressive as they are today, it is thought that there were originally some 500 frescoes here.

Mirror Wall and the Summit

Climb past the **Mirror Wall**, a dense spider's web of ancient graffiti left by visitors to the rock over the past 1,500 years, on the way to the **summit**. This involves scrambling up a crude staircase cut into the rock – but at least it has a handrail. This climb is not for the faint-hearted, but the view of the water gardens below and surrounding jungle is breathtaking. Amid the foundations and fragmentary remains of the palace is a large tank cut from the solid rock: water was brought to the summit using a typically ingenious hydraulic system driven by windmills.

Popham Arboretum

Drive back to the main A6 highway and head south in the direction of Dambulla for a further 24km (15 miles), where you will see a road to the east signposted to the Heritance Kandalama Hotel. About 3km (2 miles) along it is the **Popham Arboretum** ❻ (Thur–Tue 9am–9pm; charge). This comprises 14 hectares (35 acres) of ghostly dry tropical forest, criss-crossed by well-maintained walking trails.

It was established in 1963 by British resident Sam Popham as a reaction to the widespread logging of forests. Almost 50 years on, the arboretum has sprouted more than 70 species of precious tropical trees such as ebony, rosewood and satinwood, and attracted plentiful bird life and wildlife, making it perfect for a late morning stroll. The **Café Kanchana**, see ❶❻, at the **Heritance Kandalama Hotel** (which clings to the side of a cliff overlooking a lake) is a good spot for a light lunch.

After lunch, return to the A6 to drive northwards back to your hotel to relax by the pool at the end of a fulfilling day out, or turn south for Kandy or Colombo.

Food and Drink 🍴

❻ CAFÉ KANCHANA

Heritance Kandalama Hotel, Dambulla; tel: 066-555 5000; www.heritancehotels.com; daily 10am–8pm; $$$
Situated on the fifth floor of this iconic, modernist hotel, the Café Kanchana offers breathtaking views of the Knuckles mountain range, Sigiriya rock and the Kandalama tank. Serves snacks all day, including the signature jumbo sandwich.

MINNERIYA AND POLONNARUWA

The A6 from Colombo to Trincomalee meets the A11, bound for Polonnaruwa and the east coast, at Habarana Junction, making Habarana an ideal starting point for an exciting one-day drive through elephant country and ancient ruins.

From **Habarana ❶**, where you may have spent the previous night, start early for a day of riding and seeing elephants, as well as strolling through the ruins in the parkland around Polonnaruwa. The 43km (27-mile) stretch of road from the Habarana junction to Polonnaruwa is one of the loneliest in the area, and it is not unusual to see wild animals, including deer, monkeys and iguanas, along its length. Now a quiet town, Polonnaruwa was at its zenith of power and glory in the 11th century and was the island's capital city for 200 years.

ELEPHANT VOYAGE

Before setting out, drop into **Elephant Voyage** (Dambulla Road, Habarana; tel: 066-227 0106; daily 6am–7pm; charge) for a one-hour elephant ride around the countryside. The company has operated with tourist-board approval, and full insurance for guests, since 1993. You could also book an afternoon jeep safari here (from 3pm for three hours; charge) to visit the Minneriya and Kaudulla National Parks with expert trackers.

> **DISTANCE** 42km (26 miles)
> **TIME** A leisurely day
> **START** Habarana
> **END** Polonnaruwa
> **POINTS TO NOTE**
> Shoes and hats must be removed before entering the ancient temples and dagobas of Polonnaruwa, even though they are in ruins. After this tour, you could spend another night in Habarana, then drive south through Kandy for tours 7 and 8, exploring the hill country.

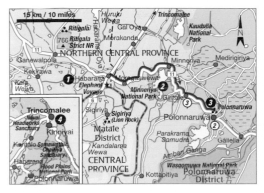

Above from left:
land monitors roam
the route to Polon-
naruwa; elephants
converge at
Minneriya; colourfully
painted bus.

MINNERIYA NATIONAL PARK

Drive northwards to the Habarana Junction to join the A11 to Polonnaruwa and the east coast. At the 32km (20-mile) marker, a car park on the southern side of the road marks the entrance to the **Minneriya National Park ❷** (daily 6am–6.30pm; charge). It is best to visit the park very early in the morning or after 3pm to see the most wildlife. The fascinating **museum** (daily 6am–6.30pm; free) is also worth seeing for its wildlife relics, including elephant and lake-crocodile skeletons.

Elephant Gathering

During the dry season, as rivers and lakes dry up across the surrounding areas and waterholes turn to baked mud, more than 300 elephants converge on the retreating waters of the Minneriya Tank, part of the park. This **Elephant Gathering** is the largest of its kind in Asia. It takes place from July to October

every year, and is at its best during August and September. However, wild elephants can be seen year-round in the park and even beside the road.

POLONNARUWA

On the road to Polonnaruwa, look out for unusual yellow road signs warning of land monitors crossing the road. They are cute to watch as they scuttle away from approaching traffic. About 1.5km (1 mile) before **Polonnaruwa ❸**, the remains of ancient ruins and centuries-old brick walls suddenly come into view on both sides of the road.

Polonnaruwa Rest House

Continue until you reach the turning south towards the **Polonnaruwa Rest House**, see ⑪①. The rest house, on the banks of an enormous lake, became famous after Queen Elizabeth II spent a night there in 1954. It's a good idea to have a light lunch here before setting out to see the ruins. The newly caught freshwater fish that sometimes feature on the menu are delicious.

Parakrama Samudra

The lake overlooked by the rest house is the **Parakrama Samudra ❹** (Sea of Parakrama), a vast reservoir of water covering 2,430 hectares (6,000 acres). King Parakramabahu (1153–86), who was responsible for this monumental feat of engineering, proclaimed that not one drop of water should escape

Stock Up
Distances between
destinations are not
long on this tour, but
because there are no
restaurants among the
ruins, you might need
to take some bottles
of water and
refreshments with you.

Food and Drink 🍽

① POLONNARUWA REST HOUSE
Polonnaruwa; tel: 027-222 2299; www.ceylonhotels.lk; daily; $$
Sri Lanka's most famous rest house, due to its idyllic lakeside location, famous guests and its restaurant poised low over the water, ideal for rice and curry, fish or a beer on its breezy veranda.

into the ocean without it being of some service to man. Today, as it was in ancient times, the reservoir is the lifeblood of the region, providing precious irrigation water for some 7,365 hectares (18,200 acres) of paddy land.

Statue of Parakramabahu/Agastaya

Before inspecting the ruins, drive south along the road (known as Pothgul Mawatha or Bund Road) constructed on top of the lake's embankment. After about 1.5km (1 mile), opposite the lake on the eastern side a small gate opens into a park (daily; free) dedicated to a huge **statue B** of a man holding a scroll carved on a rock. This 12th-century sculpture of great craftsmanship is thought to be either King Parakramabahu or Agastaya, an Indian religious teacher.

Royal Palace

Return along Bund Road to the **Visitor Information Centre** (daily; 7am–6pm) and **Museum C** (daily; 9am–5pm; charge) beside the embankment, next to the canal, to purchase a ticket to view the ruins; that's if you don't already have a Cultural Triangle Permit *(see p.64)*. As you enter the main archaeological site, the impressive remains of King Parakramabahu's **Royal Palace D** (Vejayanta Pasada) are to the right. Of the original seven floors, only three remain. A staircase leads nowhere, but its former grandeur can be imagined.

In front of it is the **Council Chamber**, restored by the British. Some fine elephant carvings have been preserved, but even the best craftsmen make mistakes – look for the five-legged elephant near one of the entrances.

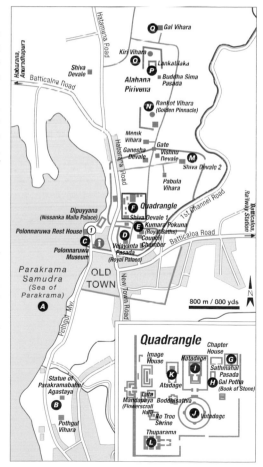

Tank Bath
The sight of people washing themselves and their clothes in the lake by the road embankment may tempt you to jump in and swim. However, only do this in the areas designated for swimming where a lifeguard is on duty.

Royal Bath

Nearby are the remains of the **Kumara Pokuna** Ⓔ (Royal Baths), an exquisite stepped bath of cut stone. Underground stone conduits feed it with water from the Parakrama Samudra. Only two of the original five crocodile spouts for water are still intact.

The Quadrangle

A number of ruins are concentrated in the **Quadrangle** Ⓕ, a short walk to the north. Climb the steps to the **Sathmahal Pasada** Ⓖ (Seven-Storey Dagoba) on the right. Its former seven floors show a distinct influence from Burma, where King Parakramabahu established meaningful contacts.

Next to the Sathmahal Pasada is the massive 9m (30ft) long **Gal Potha** Ⓗ (Book of Stone), one of the longest and heaviest of its kind in the world. The enormous slab of stone, 1.5m (5ft) wide and over 60cm (2ft) thick, is inscribed with the great achievements of Parakramabahu's successor and nephew, Nissankamalla, who indulged in an orgy of monument- and temple-building in a bid to outdo his uncle. A footnote reveals that the Stone Book was brought from Mihintale, over 100km (60 miles) away. The 25-ton book is believed to have been transported to its present site on wooden rollers tugged by elephants.

Nearby is the modest **Hatadage** Ⓘ, where the tooth of the Buddha was once housed. Built by King Nissankamalla, its columns are adorned by erotic carvings. To prevent destruction by Hindu adventurers, the king had bulls carved at the entrance, but his precaution failed to work.

Directly opposite the Hatadage is the beautiful **Vatadage** Ⓙ, a circular relic house and probably the oldest building in Polonnaruwa. Built by Parakramabahu and subsequently embellished by Nissankamalla, it is perhaps the most ornate building in Sri Lanka, its outer walls carved with friezes of lions, dwarfs and lotuses, and, at each of the four entrances, elaborate moonstones

East-Coast Season

It is only 85km (53 miles) from the Habarana Junction along the almost straight A6 to the east-coast harbour town of Trincomalee. The best time to visit the broad golden sands of the beaches of Uppuveli and Nilaveli, to the north of Trincomalee's huge bay, is between May and October, when the island's west-coast beaches suffer from the monsoon. After years of being unofficially off-limits because of the civil war, the east coast is opening up, with hotels being renovated for the tourist boom – like the former Club Oceanic, renamed as the Chaaya Blu.

Trincomalee has one of the largest and finest deep-water anchorages in the world, and was the island's main port during the Polonnaruwa era. It was coveted by the Danish, Dutch, Portuguese, French and British, not to mention the Japanese, who bombed it in 1942. The centrepiece of Trinco, as it is familiarly known, is Fort Frederick, originally built by the Portuguese in 1623, and still used by the military. There is a venerable hotel, Welcombe Inn, overlooking the harbour, as well as many guesthouses along the beaches.

and guardstones (depicting *nagaraja* – King cobra figures with seven-hooded heads, believed to prevent evil from entering the premises). Steps lead up to the central shrine, presided over by four Buddhas facing the cardinal points, and a central brick dagoba.

On the other side of the Hatadage are the fragmentary remains of the **Atadage** , built by King Parakramabahu's predecessor, King Vijayabahu, which once also housed the Buddha's tooth. The altar opposite the Buddha image is believed to be where King Nissanka-malla listened to Buddhist discourses.

The **Thuparama** temple, the only building in the Quadrangle with a roof, contains nine statues of the Buddha. One is broken but others, made of quartz and containing mica, glisten magically. Light a candle and the wonders of Thuparama are revealed. One statue is believed to have had gems embedded as eyes. They emitted strange rays when sunlight streaked in from specially constructed angled crevices.

Shiva Devale

Leave the Quadrangle, head north and turn right at the first crossroads towards the **Shiva Devale** , a circular relic house where the *yoni* and *lingum*, symbols of fertility, are worshipped by Hindu women seeking blessings for conception. Return to your vehicle and drive north to the **Rankot Vihara** (Golden Pinnacle), a colossal red-brick dagoba standing 40m (125ft) high with

a circumference of 170m (550ft). The remains of the **Alahana Pirivena** (university) and the **Royal Burial Grounds** are located nearby.

Kiri Vihara

Drive to the car park and alight to visit the well-preserved **Kiri** (Milk) **Vihara** , a dagoba named for the milk-white stucco that once covered the entire dome, and the image house, **Lankatilaka** , which has thick 17m (56ft) walls and a headless statue of the standing Buddha. Across the road is the **Gal Vihara** (Rock Temple), where a quartet of statues of the Buddha, carved out of sheer rock, are the exquisite work of 11th-century craftsmen.

It's now time for afternoon tea. Try the **Sudu Araliya Hotel**, see 🍴②, in the new town of Polonnaruwa 1km (½ mile) south, or drive back along the A11 for 8km (5 miles) to Giritale with its lovely **Deer Park Hotel**, see 🍴③.

Above from far left: the ancient Vatadage; visiting the Gal Vihara rock sculptures.

Food and Drink 🍴

② SUDU ARALIYA HOTEL
New Town, Polonnaruwa; tel: 027-222 4849; www.hotelsuduaraliya.com; daily; $$
A bright, welcoming place with views of its garden swimming pool and lake beyond. Set menus, buffets and afternoon tea served on request.

③ DEER PARK HOTEL
Giratale, Polonnaruwa; tel: 027-224 7685; www.angsana.com; daily 7.30am–10pm; $$$
Carefully crafted to blend in with its rural setting, this hotel has many corners in the garden or on wooden railed verandas in which to enjoy afternoon tea and scrumptious cakes.

GALLE FORT

Step back in time with a morning walk around magical Galle Fort, first built five centuries ago and now home of fashionable boutique shops and designer hotels created out of abandoned mansions. Later, spend a leisurely afternoon or more at one of the world's best beaches, Unawatuna.

DISTANCE 3km (2 miles)
TIME A leisurely day
START Galle Fort
END Unawatuna
POINTS TO NOTE

Galle Fort is 116km (72 miles) from Colombo and easily reached by rail or road before going on by road to Unawatuna beach. From Unawatuna it is a drive of 181km (112 miles) along the south coast to visit Yala National Park (tour 12). There is no shade along the ramparts of Galle Fort, so to shield yourself from the sun, wear a hat, or copy Sri Lankans and use an umbrella as a sun parasol.

Food and Drink 🍴

① AMANGALLA
10 Church Street; tel: 091-239 2118; daily 11am–11pm; $$
This hotel's veranda is ideal for a lime soda, coffee or beer in a fashionable, genteel atmosphere, overlooking Church Street and the grass embankments of the ramparts opposite.

Wonderwalls
The Dutch built the walls to withstand enemy cannonballs. More than 300 years later, the fort's walls did a sterling job of keeping the 2004 tsunami at bay.

Galle is the most perfectly preserved colonial town in Sri Lanka, and an atmospheric piece of time-warped island history, with streets of low-slung Dutch villas hemmed in by massive coral bastions and the breaking waves of the Indian Ocean just beyond.

History's influence is unavoidable in Galle Fort, a Unesco World Heritage Site. The peninsula forming the western wing of Galle's natural harbour was originally a low-country settlement ruled by the kings of Kandy. The Portuguese invaded in 1589, and built a fortalice overlooking the harbour. They were chased out in 1640 by the Dutch, who, during their 156 years of occupation, added major fortifications and enclosed the peninsula.

MAIN GATE

Entrance is through the **Main Gate** ❶, just 250m/yds from the railway and bus stations and overlooking the Test cricket stadium. The gate was created by the British in 1873 by tunnelling through the embankment that links the western Star Bastion with the

eastern Sun Bastion. The clock tower that looms over the central Moon Bastion was added in 1881.

CHURCH STREET

After emerging through the gateway tunnel, take Church Street to the east where it curves below the rampart wall. The long, whitewashed building is the **Galle National Museum** ❷ (Tue–Sat 9am–5pm, charge), originally part of the complex built by the Dutch in 1684 to house army officers.

Immediately past here lies the superbly renovated **Amangalla** hotel, see ⑪① (the successor of the famous old New Oriental House), occupying a three-storey Regency-style building.

Groote Kerk

Evidence of the past is to be seen in the solid form of the tombstones of Dutch and British residents in the cemetery garden of **Groote Kerk** ❸ (Great Church) at the corner of Middle Street, adjoining to the hotel. This Dutch Reformed church dates

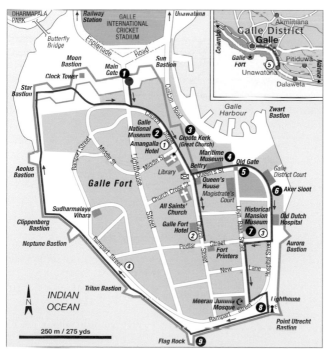

Above from left:
a young diver at Flag
Rock; Dutch-era
architecture recalls a
bygone age; stopping
for a rest.

from 1755 and is the oldest Protestant
place of worship in Sri Lanka. Look
up across the road at the corner of
Queen's Street to see the **belfry** tower,
built in 1701.

A little further along, on the other
side of the street, is the British-era **All
Saints' Church**, and just beyond it is
an amazing hotel, the **Galle Fort**, see
①②, created in 2005 out of an abandoned mansion dating back to 1695.
Also on the street, houses of colonial
Dutch and British Art Deco design
have been transformed into boutique
shops bursting with designer goodies.

Unawatuna Beach

Five km (3 miles) beyond Galle lies the picture-perfect bay
and endearing little village of Unawatuna – the most popular beachside hangout in Sri Lanka, and deservedly so.
Long a favourite with backpackers, the village manages to
strike just the right balance between crashed-out beachside somnolence and a splash of party atmosphere,
particularly during the season – and it's a pleasant contrast
to the much more organised and orderly tourist resorts
along the west coast. There is reasonable swimming (and
a little bit of live coral) in the sheltered bay – and dolphin-
spotting too – although encroaching development has
reduced the beach in places to a narrow ribbon of sand,
and from December to April it is packed with people.

Rooms, food (and drink) are available right on the beach,
and there are dozens of guesthouses in the lanes leading
off it as well as one star-class hotel, the Unawatuna Beach
Resort. The popular restaurant called Lucky Tuna, run by
the amiable Lalith and his family, has added four upstairs
rooms with breathtaking balcony views of the entire bay.

QUEEN'S STREET

Retrace your steps for a few yards then
turn right down Queen's Street where
the **Queen's House** opposite the
belfry boldly displays the date ANNO
1683. The road runs beside the
restored Dutch spice warehouse that
forms part of the fort's wall, and now
houses the **Maritime Museum** ❹
(Tue–Sat 9am–5pm; charge). The
museum features replicas of old boats,
ranging from Moorish trading vessels
to British naval ships, as well as the
carcass of a whale, which dangles from
the ceiling of the main room.

This adjoins the fort's **Old Gate** ❺,
which has the novelty of two competing crests: the VOC (Dutch) crest
dated ANNO MDCLXIX is above
the gate on the inside of the fort,
while the British coat of arms has
been added above the gate on the outside wall. Look closely, though, and
you will see the VOC crest and date
1668 are also there.

AKER SLOOT

Walk back through the gate into the
fort and skirt round the paved town
square (it used to be a green) to the
eastern corner, where the date 1759
etched into a white wall identifies the
Aker Sloot ❻. Still a government
residence, the breadfruit tree above its
high walls was introduced by the Dutch
as the first of its kind on the island.

The long white building on the rampart side while walking along Hospital Street is the old **Dutch Hospital**. Opposite, the **Thenu Rest**, see ⑪③, offers refreshments on demand.

Historical Mansion Museum
Behind the Thenu Rest, on Leyn Baan Street, is the **Historical Mansion Museum** ❼ (daily 9am–6pm, closed Friday noon–2pm), a well-laid-out commercial establishment where most of the ancient artefacts, bric-a-brac and jewellery on display can be bought.

THE RAMPARTS

South of here, Leyn Baan Street continues to the seafront ramparts and the 18m (59ft) **lighthouse** ❽ at the Point Utrecht Bastion, built in 1940 to replace the old British lighthouse that burnt down in 1936. While you can't climb it, you can step up to the top of the rampart wall and walk along the grass embankment. On the landside is the white, Gothic-looking **Meeran Jumma Mosque**. At **Flag Rock** ❾ eager youths dive 20m (65ft) into the tiny pool hemmed in by rocks in the sea below.

From here, you can walk along the embankment parallel to Rampart Street with the sea on one side and the red-tiled rooftops of the tiny houses crammed into the fort on the other. One of these, called **Pilgrim's Lounge**, see ⑪④, is now a bohemian-style café. Opposite are steps down from the ramparts to pockets of beach where families splash in the sea and couples smooch under umbrellas.

After the **Aeolus Bastion**, the ramparts broaden and provide a breezy walk past the **Star Bastion** to the **clock tower** and back to the Main Gate.

UNAWATUNA

A ride by three-wheeler taxi for 5km (3 miles) east along the south coast will bring you to **Unawatuna** beach *(see feature)* for lunch at **Lucky Tuna**, see ⑪⑤, and a swim to end the day's outing.

Flag Rock Pool
You don't need to dive to get into the rock pool – it's fun to swim there or snorkel in its clear waters from the tiny beach around the corner. Watch out, though, for boys plunging down from above.

Food and Drink

② GALLE FORT HOTEL
28 Church Street; tel: 091-223 2870; daily 11am–11pm; $$$
Enjoy the eccentricities and colonial grace and charm of this hotel over a drink and a delectable Thai-style set lunch on its veranda or in the bar.

③ THENU REST
12 Hospital Street; tel: 091-224 6608; daily 9am–9pm; $
A small (only four rooms, one of which has AC), very clean guesthouse in a quiet lane. It has a small lounge for snacks and soft drinks, and free Internet service for residents.

④ PILGRIM'S LOUNGE
31B Rampart Street; tel: 077-698 0257; daily 9am–10pm; $
A bright, bohemian atmosphere in this small, informally run café beside the rampart wall at the southern edge of Galle Fort. Good for short eats.

⑤ LUCKY TUNA
Unawatuna, Galle; tel: 091-224 1629; daily 6am–midnight; $
An informal restaurant with a bar counter right on the beach, specialising in fish dishes including large, battered mixed seafood spring rolls. Perfect for a leisurely lunch, or to party the night away. Four spectacular rooms ($$).

YALA NATIONAL PARK

After touring the cities, cultural ruins and tea country, see Sri Lanka in the raw at the Yala National Park, with a jeep safari into the wild where elephants roam, leopards lurk, crocodiles gape and peacocks strut.

DISTANCE 67km (42 miles)
TIME A full day
START Hambantota
END Yala National Park
POINTS TO NOTE

The best way to visit the park is to take an early jeep tour at around 6am to view bird life, or at around 3pm for elephants. Leopards can sometimes be seen, but sloth bears are elusive. The park is closed every year from 1 September to 16 October, when animals move elsewhere in search of water. This tour follows tour 11 if you take the A2 for 128km (80 miles) east from Galle; or after tour 8 drive 88km (55 miles) south from Ella on the A23/A2 to pick it up at Tissamaharama.

Park Formalities

To visit Yala National Park, you will have to hire a jeep and a tracker, as well as pay an admission fee per person and per vehicle. Jeep safaris cost less the nearer you stay to the park. Be prepared for a long wait at the security checkpoint about 1km (½ mile) before the park entrance for your passport details to be laboriously copied in a ledger by hand; no passport, no entry.

Food and Drink

① HAMBANTOTA REST HOUSE

Hambantota; tel: 047-222 0299; daily noon–3pm, 7–10pm; $$

An independently run government rest house with a charming view of the fishing harbour and sand dunes beyond. The à la carte menu offers fresh fish dishes such as devilled or fried seer or whole fish curry.

Of Sri Lanka's 20 national parks, the most famous is Yala National Park (officially called Ruhuna National Park), which covers a vast swathe of countryside in the southeast of the island beyond Tissamaharama. Much of the park is closed to visitors, but the area which is open has probably the richest and most varied collection of wildlife in the country, including a substantial elephant population, elusive sloth bears, gorgeous bird life and, most famously, a significant leopard population. Although they're not easy to spot, you've reasonable odds of seeing one if you spend some time in the park with a reputable outfit. Yala is the best park in the country for viewing the biggest variety of mammals in a single day.

The park was established in 1899, having previously been a shooting reserve. It covers 1,295 sq km (500 square miles): the western block, open to visitors, consists of 14,100 hectares (34,843 acres) and was declared a National Park in 1938. With a diverse range of habitats including scrub jungle, tanks, brackish lagoons and swamps, the flora is typical of dry-season monsoon forest.

HAMBANTOTA

From Galle as you reach the salt pans at **Hambantota** ❶ (128 km/50 miles from Galle) you will see signs of the massive developments for a major new port and a second international airport taking place. Turn off the new highway that bypasses Hambantota to drive into the town, one of the largest on the south coast. The town has Sri Lanka's largest population of Malay Muslims – its name is said to derive from *sampans*, the boats that the Malays arrived in, and *tota*, or harbour. You will notice an unusually large number of mosques here, as well as the occasional decidedly oriental-looking face amid the Sri Lankan crowds. It's also known as the island's major centre of salt produc-tion, which is collected from the enormous evaporating salt pans that ring the town, and for its curd, made from buffalo milk, and sold from many roadside stalls – look for the strings of clay pots hanging up outside local shops. For refreshment try the **Hambantota Rest House**, see ⑪①.

TISSAMARAHAMA

Return to the coastal road to drive through lush, low vegetation that gives way to thorny plants and small shrubs, typical of the dry zone. After 15km (9 miles) the road passes **Bundala National Park**, one of the country's finest and famed for its bird life, and gradually turns inland towards **Tissamaharama** ❷ (or 'Tissa', as it's usually

Above from far left: chital (spotted deer) at Yala; blue sky and an empty road.

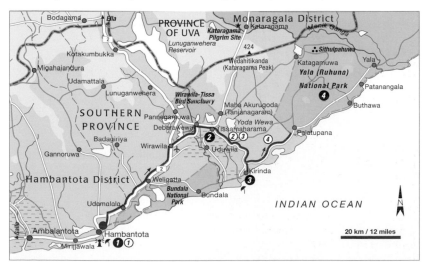

called), one of the most historic towns in the south. Under the name of Mahagama it formerly served as the capital of southern Sri Lanka during the Anuradhapuran period, and still has a pair of huge stupas and a collection of ancient tanks (man-made lakes).

Safari Jeeps

Turn east into town and you will soon be waved to a stop by young men wanting to arrange a safari jeep for you. If you are not going to stay close to the gates of the park, stop at the car park beside the lake where a huge sign advertises the **Independent Safari Jeep Association** (2 Punchi Akurugoda; tel: 047-567 1480; email: isja_yala@yahoo.com; daily 5.30am–6pm; charge), an organisation with over 150 jeeps for hire. Motorboats to tour the lake can also be hired here.

There are many guesthouses that offer refreshments in the town, with popular choices being the lakeside **Tissamaharama Resort**, see Ⓨ②, and the nearby **Refresh Hotel**, see Ⓨ③.

KIRINDA

To reach the Yala National Park, set off southwards towards the coast along the road to Kirinda, 10km (6 miles) away. You pass another hotel catering for tourists, the **Elephant Reach**, on the north side close to the lake. At **Kirinda** ❸ there is a lovely view of the southern coast from a temple atop a rock. This

is the spot where Vihara Mahadevi, the mother of the Sinhala hero Dutugemunu, is said to have landed. She had been sent out to sea on a boat as a sacrifice by her father, King Kelanitissa of Kelaniya, to placate angry gods.

Signs of human habitation become sparse as the road winds for another 33km (21 miles) along the coast through scrubland, salt pans and swamps where buffaloes wallow. Watch out for peacocks preening themselves and the grey silhouettes of wild elephants, looking like boulders, in the distance. Just before the entrance to the park is a signpost to **Yala Village**, see Ⓨ④, the only hotel close to the park and the most convenient place to stay or have a meal. Safaris can be arranged with the drivers of jeeps parked at the hotel's gate.

YALA NATIONAL PARK

After checking in, it's a good time for an afternoon safari. By hired jeep it takes about 10 minutes to drive to the **Yala National Park** ❹ (information: Department of Wildlife Conservation, 18 Gregory's Road, Colombo; tel: 011-226 9421; daily 6.30am–6.30pm, except Sept–mid-Oct; charge). There is a small museum near the entrance showing the development of the park, as well as models and skeletons of animals found there.

In addition to the entrance fee, you have to pay a tracker assigned by the park. The trackers are experienced in

Above: painted stork; safari snapper.

Kataragama

About 29km (18 miles) north of Tissa, Kataragama is one of the holiest sites on the island, held sacred by Buddhists, Hindus and Muslims alike. Pilgrims come here all year round to worship at the shrine of the god Kataragama Deviyo. The temple complex stands on one side of the Menik river, where an extensive collection of shrines and temples lies scattered around a beautiful area of wooded parkland.

the ways of the jungle and usually prove to be fascinating companions. The tracker will indicate the places to find wildlife, including herds of deer, buffaloes, crocodiles, sambhurs, monkeys, flying squirrels and birds that migrate from India and as far afield as Europe, such as painted stork, heron, ibis, green bee-eater, green pigeon and even the Malabar pied hornbill. These spots are usually near waterholes, where the animals come to drink in the evening and early morning.

Elephants and Leopards

The greatest thrill, though, is the sight of wild elephants and leopards. The elephant found in Sri Lanka belongs to the same subspecies as that found throughout Asia. These huge creatures move majestically and are seldom bothered about visitors, except when they feel threatened. Leopards are quite rare at Yala – spotting one would be the highlight of an adventure in the park. A persistent tracker sometimes finds one, usually seen playing like an overgrown cat on the road.

Night in the Jungle

Return to the Yala Village at dusk for a sundowner on the upper deck of the bar, from where you can sometimes see animals roaming, or drive back to your Tissamaharama base. The jeep will return for you at 5.30am the next day for another three-hour visit to the park. If you fancy a night in the jungle and

want to see more animals, including leopards, small Indian civets and other nocturnal animals like the pangolin, porcupine and slender loris, it is possible to tour the park in a custom-built 4WD Land Cruiser and dine in the wild. The night is spent in specially erected tents, complete with a hot and cold shower and a chemical toilet. **Leopard Safaris**, run by a Sri Lankan wildlife enthusiast, offer an experience of the true wild in uncompromised luxury (Noel Rodrigo, Leopard Safaris Pvt Ltd, Negombo; tel: 077-731 4004; www.leopardsafaris.com)

Food and Drink

② TISSAMAHARAMA RESORT
Tissamaharama; tel: 047-223 7299; www.ceylonhotels.lk; daily 12.30–2.30pm, 7.30–10.30pm; $$
With a view of the lake and bird life, this is a popular restaurant, even if you're not staying here, for a buffet or set-menu lunch and dinner. Lake fish is a speciality.

③ REFRESH HOTEL
Akurugoda, Tissamaharama; tel: 047-223 7357; www.refreshrestaurant.com; daily 7.30am–10.30pm; $$
Set in a tropical garden, this is the sister restaurant of the popular one on the west coast at Hikkaduwa (see p.107). It offers Western, Eastern, Chinese, seafood and vegetarian dishes, as well as snacks like stuffed eggplant and mushroom puffs. Service is swift and friendly and there is also a bar.

④ YALA VILLAGE
Kirinda, Tissamaharama; tel: 047-223 9449; www.johnkeellshotels.com; daily 7–10.30am, 12.30–2.30pm, 7.30–10.30pm; $$$
A resort in the jungle where elephants often pop in, this hotel serves snacks in its poolside air-conditioned lounge bar, and buffets with a wide selection of Western and Eastern dishes in the first-floor open-sided restaurant with jungle views.

DIRECTORY

A user-friendly alphabetical listing of practical information, plus hand-picked hotels and restaurants, clearly organised by area, to suit all budgets and tastes.

A

ADMISSION CHARGES

Entry fees to state-sponsored institutions like museums, the zoo and the elephant orphanage are based on a two-tier system: tourists pay up to 20 times more than Sri Lankans or foreigners with resident visas. Fees are quoted in US dollars but payable in Sri Lanka rupees. There is no charge for temples, except Kandy's Temple of the Tooth.

When visiting sites in the Cultural Triangle, it is advisable to obtain a combination ticket for US$50. This includes charges for photography and admission to Sigiriya, Anuradhapura and Polonnaruwa. Individual tickets for each site are US$25. Tickets are available at each site, or at the Cultural Triangle Office, 212/1 Bauddhaloka Mawatha, Colombo 7, tel: 011-258 7912.

AGE RESTRICTIONS

To qualify for reduced entry charges, children need to be under 12. To drive you must be over 18; to drink and go to casinos, at least 18.

B

BEGGING

Sri Lankans, who believe to give is to earn merit, will spare a coin to those they see as genuine beggars. Beggars deliberately target tourists, so if you are feeling compassionate, donate to a suitable charity instead.

BUDGETING

It is still possible to find single B&B in a village guesthouse for around Rs1,500 a night, and it would be possible to eat in basic cafés on Rs1,000 a day. However, budget more than that for comfort and better food, extras like bottled mineral water (Rs50), soft drinks (Rs35), touring (allow Rs10,000 a day for hired vehicle with driver), high admission charges and unexpected splurges (like medical treatment, a hotel buffet dinner or buying gems).

C

CHILDREN

Sri Lankans adore children and make a great deal of fuss over them, and children happily enjoy the country. Baby food and nappies are available in major supermarkets but are expensive.

CLOTHING

Cottons and light natural fabrics such as linen are ideal in the lowland heat. Skimpy skirts and brief shorts are not considered respectable, and will attract stares and a certain amount of hassle. For women, loose cotton skirts or

trousers and tops, and a long dress or skirt and long-sleeved blouse for visiting temples are ideal. Men will feel comfortable in cotton trousers or shorts and a T-shirt. For climate details, *see p.12*.

CRIME AND SAFETY

Sri Lanka is a reassuringly safe country. Nevertheless, exercise caution and common sense. Never flash valuables or leave them lying around.

The most obvious safety hazard is traffic, since vehicles often behave in unexpected and potentially dangerous ways. If you're cycling, take extra care. Swimming in the sea can be dangerous because of currents; only swim where others are bathing.

The following websites publish up-to-date travel advisories: www.fco.gov.uk; www.travel.state.gov/travel_warnings; www.smartraveller.gov.au.

CUSTOMS

If you are bringing in over US$10,000 in cash or traveller's cheques, or valuable gems and jewellery, this should be declared at customs on arrival, to avoid problems when leaving. Duty-free allowances permit up to 1.5 litres of spirits, 2 bottles of wine, and perfume in a quantity for personal use. There is no duty-free allowance for tobacco products. Drugs are illegal, and possession could carry the death penalty.

On Departure

Customs officers may check your luggage for items being taken out of the country without a permit. The export of 'antiques' (defined as anything over 50 years old) is prohibited without a special licence, as is the export of native fauna and flora.

Unused Sri Lankan currency should be reconverted into foreign currency (so keep all foreign-exchange transaction receipts to prove you acquired Sri Lankan currency with foreign currency).

DISABLED TRAVELLERS

Sri Lanka is not well equipped for those with physical disabilities. Only a few of the five-star hotels have access and facilities for people in wheelchairs – public transport has none. Wheelchairs are available at the international airport on prior request through the airlines.

E

ELECTRICITY

Sri Lanka uses 230–240 volts, 50 cycles, alternating current. Most sockets are three-pronged both square and round; adaptors are cheap and readily available from hardware shops. Power often fluctuates, even in the cities.

Above from far left: Buddha at the Seema Malakaya, Colombo; Sri Lankan flag.

EMBASSIES AND HIGH COMMISSIONS

Australia. Australian High Commission; 21 Gregory's Road, Colombo 7, tel: 011-246 3200; www.srilanka. embassy.gov.au

Canada. High Commission of Canada; 33A 5th Lane, Colombo 3, tel: 011-532 6232; www.canadainternational.gc.ca/ sri_lanka

New Zealand. New Zealand High Commission, New Delhi, India, is accredited to Sri Lanka; www.nz embassy.com

South Africa. South African High Commission; 114 Rosmead Place, Colombo 7, tel: 011-268 9926

UK. British High Commission; 389 Bauddhaloka Mawatha, Colombo 7, tel: 011-539 0639; http://ukinsrilanka. fco.gov.uk/en

USA. Embassy of the United States; 210 Galle Road, Colombo 3, tel: 011-249 8500; http://srilanka.us embassy.gov

EMERGENCIES

Accident Service: 011-269 1111
Fire and Ambulance: 011-242 2222
Police: 119 from landline, 112 if dialled from mobile phone
Tourist Police: Anuradhapura 025-222 4546; Bentota 034-227 5022; Colombo 011-242 1451; Hikkaduwa 091-227 7222; Polonnaruwa 027-222 3099

ETIQUETTE

While Sri Lankans eat rice and curry with their right hand, visitors may feel more comfortable using a spoon and fork. When handing objects to another person, either the right hand or both hands should be used.

Skimpy clothing should be confined to the beach or pool area; modest, conservative dress is appropriate elsewhere. Many Sri Lankans, including monks, do not shake hands and should be greeted with palms held together at chest height and a bow of the head.

Waggling the head from side to side is not a negative gesture but a sign that the matter is being considered.

If you are invited to eat in a Sri Lankan village home, don't be surprised if the women keep hidden and don't eat with you. They, and the rest of the family, will eat after you've finished. In Colombo, however, women see themselves as equal to their male colleagues.

G

GAY/LESBIAN ISSUES

Homosexuality is illegal in Sri Lanka, so discretion is advised.

GREEN ISSUES

There is no high awareness of green issues in the country, except among visitors who are careful with what they

Carbon Offsetting

Air travel produces a huge amount of carbon dioxide and is a significant contributor to global warming. If you would like to offset the damage caused to the environment by your flight, a number of organisations do this, using online 'carbon calculators', which tell you how much you need to donate. In the UK travellers can visit www.climatecare. org or www. carbonneutral.com; in the US log on to www.climatefriendly. com or www. sustainabletravel international.org.

do with their rubbish. However, some hotels (especially Heritance Kandalama and Heritance Tea Factory, *see p.100 and p.102*) are pioneers in creating energy from bio fuels, organic gardening and dedicated recycling.

HEALTH

Inoculations

Proof of immunisation is not normally required, unless you have passed through an infected area within 14 days prior to your arrival. Anti-malaria tablets prescribed by your doctor should be started about a week before you plan to arrive.

Healthcare and Insurance

The Sri Lankan health service does not provide free treatment for visitors, so insurance is vital.

Hospitals

Private doctors and good private hospitals are to be found in Colombo and tourist areas. Private hospitals are generally well run and comfortable. In Colombo, these include the **Apollo**, 578 Elvitigala Mawatha, Colombo 5, tel: 011-543 0000; the **Nawaloka**, 23 Sri Sugathodaya Mawatha, Colombo 2, tel: 011-254 4444; and **Oasis**, 18A M. E. D. Dabare Mawatha, Narahenpita, Colombo 5, tel: 011-236 9113; in Galle, the **Ruhunu** Hospital, Karapitiya Road, tel: 091-223 4061.

Pharmacies

Most Western medicines are available, and so are many Indian substitutes. The Colombo branch of the state-run Osusala Pharmacy (255 Dharmapala Mawatha/Lipton Circus, Colombo 7; tel: 011-269 4716) is open 24 hours and every town has several pharmacies.

HOURS AND HOLIDAYS

Hours

Government offices, including post offices, and businesses observe a five-day working week, opening Monday to Friday from around 8.30 or 9.30am and closing around 4.30 or 5.30pm. Banks open Monday to Friday from 9 or 9.30am until 1.30 or 3.30pm; some branches also open on Saturday mornings. All shops and banks close on public holidays. Most branches of Keells and Cargills supermarkets are open 8am–8pm every day. In small towns, the shopping hours depend on the shop owner; many open late and on Sunday.

Public Holidays

Public, bank and *Poya* (full moon) holidays change every year as they are based on lunar cycles. The constant national holidays are: 4 February – National Day; 1 May – May Day; 25 December – Christmas Day.

The Muslim holidays of Id-Ul-Fitr (Ramadan Festival Day), Id-Ul-Allah (Hajji Festival Day) and Milad-Un-Nabi (Holy Prophet's Birthday) are

also national holidays celebrated on different days each year, according to the cycles of the Muslim calendar.

Other holidays usually occur in the following months:

January: Tamil Thai Pongal, Durutu Poya
February: Navan Poya
March: Mahasivarathri, Medin Poya
March/April: Good Friday
April: Day prior to Sinhalese/Tamil New Year, Sinhalese/Tamil New Year, Bak Poya
May: Vesak Poya and day after
June: Poson Poya
July: Esala Poya
August: Nikini Poya
September: Binara Poya
October: Vap Poya
October/November: Deepavali
November: Il Poya
December: Unduvap Poya

I

INTERNET FACILITIES

Internet cafés are widely found even in the smallest towns. Charges are Rs100–200 per hour.

L

LANGUAGE

The main language is Sinhala, spoken by around 75 percent of the population. Tamil is the first language of around 25 percent, as both Tamils and east-coast Muslims speak it. English is spoken well by 10 percent of the population, while many more can communicate adequately; it is the language of business and tourism. Sinhala-speakers generally respond to foreigners' attempts to speak their language with incomprehension and prefer to practise their English instead.

M

MAPS

Useful for finding your way around Colombo and the major towns is Arjuna's A–Z Street Guide, available from Colombo bookshops.

MEDIA

Newspapers
Sri Lanka has three daily English and three Sunday newspapers with island-wide circulation; these are mainly available from stalls and pavement sellers. The *Daily News* (www.daily news.lk) and the *Sunday Observer* (www.sundayobserver.lk) are state-controlled and thus serve as mouthpieces for the government. Independent newspapers include *The Island* (and *Sunday Island*; www.island.lk), and the *Daily Mirror* (www.dailymirror.lk) and its sister publication the *Sunday Times* (www.sundaytimes.lk). While international magazines such as *Newsweek* and

caption
Above from far left: National Day festivities in Negombo; Sri Lankan banknotes.

Time can be bought locally, foreign newspapers cannot. The free monthly magazine *Explore Sri Lanka* carries feature articles as well as information of interest to visitors.

Radio

There are several English-language radio stations churning out mainstream pop music and cheesy chat. The best is TNL Radio (101.7 FM; www.tnlrocks.com); others worth a listen are Yes FM (89.5 FM; www.yesfmonline.com) and Sun FM (99.9 FM).

Television

Sri Lankan television is unlikely to take up much of your time; both state and private channels broadcast mainly in Sinhala or Tamil, and what little English-language programming there is tends to be fairly dire. Satellite television is available island-wide with international news channels.

MONEY

Currency

The national currency is the Sri Lankan rupee. Coins come in denominations of one, two, five and 10 rupees, and notes in denominations of 10, 20, 50, 100, 500, 1,000 and 2,000 rupees.

Credit Cards

Most hotels, restaurants and shops accept credit cards. Visa and MasterCard are widely accepted; American Express and Diners Club less so. Be careful of credit card copying and don't allow your card out of your sight.

ATMs

There are hundreds of ATMs across the island that accept foreign Visa and/or MasterCards; every town of any consequence will have at least one such machine where there is a bank.

Exchanging Money

All banks change traveller's cheques, with Thomas Cook and American Express being the most widely recognised. The rate for traveller's cheque is better than for cash. Money can also be withdrawn on credit cards in banks, though it's generally easier and faster just to use an ATM *(see above)*.

Tipping

Most hotels and restaurants add a 10 percent service charge to the bill; if a service charge isn't included, tip 10 percent in cash. Where the service charge is included, 5 percent in cash pressed into the palm of the person you want to have it will make certain the right one gets rewarded. Chauffeurs and guides will also expect to be tipped somewhere in the region of US$5–10 per day, depending on their skills and helpfulness. Guides who show you around temples will expect a small tip (Rs50–100 should suffice, although do not give money directly to monks, but place it in a donation box).

Religion

There are four major religions in Sri Lanka: Buddhism (practised by roughly 70 percent of the population), Hinduism (15 percent), Christianity (7 percent) and Islam (7 percent). Almost all Sinhalese are Buddhist (there is a small number of Christian Sinhalese). The majority of Tamils are Hindu, though there are also significant numbers of Tamil Christians.

P

POLICE

Sri Lankan police are generally friendly with foreigners, but if you have a problem or need to report a crime, it is best to take a Sinhala-speaking local with you. There are tourist police offices in a few towns, but these have little knowledge of tourism or tourists. If you have anything stolen and want to make an insurance claim, you will need a police report. The police uniform is khaki.

POST

When sending airmail letters or cards with stamps, make sure that they are franked in front of you at the post-office counter. International courier services include the following:

DHL, 148 Vauxhall Street, Colombo 2, tel: 011-230 4304

FedEx, 93 1/1 Chatham Street, Colombo 1, tel: 011-254 4357

TNT, 315 Vauxhall Street, Colombo 2, tel: 011-230 8444

S

SMOKING

The rules are confused but generally mean you can smoke when dining out of doors, on a hotel's open-air terrace or in a restaurant's garden but, curi-ously, smoking is allowed in some hotel lounges if they have less than a speci-fied number of guests, and in casinos.

T

TELEPHONES

There are several mobile-phone service providers; a local prepaid mobile-phone account can be set up easily.

The international dialling code to contact a number in Sri Lanka is 00 94. The first digit (0) of the phone numbers given in this guide should be omitted when telephoning from over-seas. When telephoning someone in Colombo from a Colombo number, omit the 011 prefix.

TIME ZONE

Sri Lanka's clocks are set at Coordi-nated Universal Time UTC (GMT) +5½ – in other words 5½ hours ahead of GMT in winter, and 4½ hours in summer. Sri Lanka is 4½ hours behind Australia in winter and 5½ hours in summer; or 10½ hours ahead of New York in winter, and 9½ in summer.

TOILETS

Public toilets are virtually non-existent: in an emergency, head for the nearest hotel or decent pastry shop. It is pru-dent to carry a cache of toilet paper in case none is available in the loo.

TOURIST INFORMATION

The Sri Lanka Tourist Promotion Bureau has its own website with stacks of information (www.srilanka.travel). The head office is at 80 Galle Road, Colombo 3, tel: 011-243 7055, and there is a 24-hour counter in the arrivals hall (after customs) at the Colombo International Airport, tel: 011-225 2411, and in the Kandy City Centre mall (daily 8.30am–5pm), tel: 081-222 2661.

Overseas offices include these:

Australia. 29 Lonsdale Street, Braddon, ACT 2612, tel: 026 230 6002; www.srilankatourism.org **UK.** Sri Lanka Tourist Office, 1 Devonshire Square, London EC2M 4WD, tel: 0845-880 6333; www.srilanka.travel

TRANSPORT

Airports – Arrival and Departure
Sri Lankan Airlines (UL) operates daily non-stop flights between Colombo and London Heathrow and some flights via the Maldives, as well as direct from Frankfurt, Paris and Rome. Other flights from Europe necessitate a change of planes in the Middle East. As well as UL, major airlines serving Colombo include Cathay Pacific, Emirates, Ethiad, Oman, Qatar, Royal Jordanian, Singapore and Thai. The airport is also served by regular charter flights from Europe.

Colombo International Airport is bright and functions smoothly; there are duty-free shops for arriving passengers after immigration. Trolleys are available free in the luggage hall. After emerging from customs there is a lobby with banks, hotel and taxi counters and an area where people who have paid a fee (Rs150) wait to meet passengers. Book a taxi there at about Rs2,500 to Colombo. There is a walk of 100m/yds to the exit. There is no dedicated airport bus service, and the local buses are infrequent and crowded and not recommended for jet-lagged passengers.

On departure, porters are available and are worth it (Rs50 a bag) for getting you through the queues and luggage X-ray efficiently. Departure tax is included in the cost of your airline ticket.

Public Transport
With its bus and train services reaching most important points, Sri Lanka is ideal for independent touring.
Bus. Buses reach pretty much every town or village of any significance anywhere on the island, though services are often slow, crowded and uncomfortable. Government buses (usually painted orange) are incredibly cheap but stop absolutely everywhere and usually get horribly packed – best avoided except for very short journeys. Private buses come in various standards and sizes – from big old rust buckets which are similar in speed,

cost and comfort to government buses, ranging up through 'semi-express' and 'express' services, which tend to make fewer stops and thus reach destinations a bit faster. The fastest vehicles, called 'inter-city expresses', usually have air-conditioning, tinted windows and padded seats. These make only limited stops and don't accept standing passengers – at least in theory – and are more recklessly driven.

Train. Sri Lanka's antiquated railway system offers a charming – if slow – way of getting around the island, especially on the scenic hill-country line. Fares are low, though carriages can often get ridiculously overcrowded, and delays are the norm rather than the exception. There are three main lines starting from Colombo: the Coast Line runs north to Negombo and Puttalam and south to Galle and Matara (there are plans to extend this line to Kataragama); the Main Line goes east, via Kandy, to Nanu Oya and Badulla; and the Northern Line goes via Anuradhapura to Vavuniya. A side branch of the Northern Line goes to Trincomalee, while another goes to Polonnaruwa and Batticaloa. For more information contact Train Enquiries on 011-243 4215.

Taxis

As well as the ubiquitous motorised rickshaws (tuk-tuks), there are metered taxi services in Colombo, but they don't cruise or wait on the street like tuk-tuks. They have to be booked by telephone *(see below)*. Away from the capital, 'taxis' are minivans; in most towns they congregate near bus stations waiting for custom, or can be arranged through your hotel. Some taxi firms with fixed rates per km: **Ace Cabs**, tel: 011-250 1502; **GNTC**, tel: 011-268 8688; **Quick Radio Cab**, tel: 011-250 2888; **Swallow Quick Cabs**, tel: 011-537 7677; **Yellow Cabs**, tel: 011-250 2888.

Driving

Sri Lanka's anarchic traffic and idiosyncratic road rules make driving a challenge for foreigners. If you don't absolutely have to drive, the best option is to hire a car with a driver – which is often no more expensive than hiring a self-drive car. If you're determined to drive, you'll need an international driving licence, which must be endorsed by the Automobile Association of Ceylon (tel: 011-242 1528), 40 Sir Macan Markar Mawatha, just off Galle Face Green in Colombo.

Car Rental. Firms include **Avis**, Keels Tours (PVT) Ltd, 429 Ferguson Road, Colombo 15; tel: 011-252 9239; www.avis.co.uk/carhire/asia/sri-lanka/colombo; **Casons Rent-A-Car**, tel: 011 440 5070; www.casonscar.com; **Mal-Key Rent-A-Car**, tel: 011-236 5251; www.malkey.lk.

Chauffeur-Driven Cars. Cars driven by chauffeur-guides can be arranged through your hotel, or you could get a quotation from a taxi company *(see above)* for an out-of-town tour.

V

VISAS AND PASSPORTS

Nationals from more than 50 countries are given a free, 30-day visa on arrival if visiting as tourists; this can be extended, but usually for not more than 90 days. Passports must be valid for six months after arrival. Visitors coming for business purposes require a visa in advance, obtainable from their home country's Sri Lankan embassy or consulate.

Visa extensions are given at the **Department of Emigration and Immigration** (41 Ananda Rajakaruna Mawatha, Punchi Borella, Colombo 10, tel: 011-532 9300; www.immigration. gov.lk). The charge is based on what your own country charges a visiting Sri Lankan. You need an onward ticket and proof of having changed sufficient funds to support yourself while in the country, calculated at US$25 a day.

If you want to avoid bureaucracy there is a private agency that can act for genuine visa extension cases: **Migration Lanka Services**, 5a Aloe Avenue (off Galle Road), Colombo 3, tel: 011-237 5972; www.migrationlanka.com.

WEBSITES

As well as the useful websites listed elsewhere in this book, the following may also be of interest:

www.srilanka.travel – Official website of the Sri Lanka Tourism Promotion Bureau.
www.visitsrilanka.org – Travel Agents Association of Sri Lanka.
www.priu.gov.lk – Official website of the government of Sri Lanka, with links to major government departments.

WEIGHTS AND MEASURES

Sri Lanka uses the metric system; roads are marked in kilometres.

WOMEN AND SOLO TRAVELLERS

Sri Lankan society is rather traditional in outlook, and the way you dress contributes greatly to people's opinion of you, and also to the way they behave towards you. Women and solo travellers should dress conservatively (at least away from established tourist beaches) and be firm, even rude, to unwarranted attention.

Unfortunately, solo travellers, whether male or female, especially on beaches, will attract attention from male opportunists who refuse to believe you really want to be left alone. To deter them, walk away and avoid conversation – and definitely eye contact – as this is seen as encouragement. On trains or buses, be wary of the male who sits beside you when there are plenty of seats elsewhere.

Above from far left: truck bearing a heavy load; rail is a charming way to explore Sri Lanka.

There is a broad range of accommodation available throughout the country, from budget-rate guesthouses to expensive, designer-smart boutique villas.

Independent travellers can usually find walk-in accommodation or book through a local travel agent. Sri Lanka has three major local hotel chains: John Keells Hotels (www.johnkeellshotels.com), Aitken Spence Hotels (www.aitkenspencehotels.com) and Jetwing Hotels (www.jetwinghotels.com). All run their properties to a high standard.

In Colombo, accommodation and service is of a high standard. Hotels inland are generally more interesting architecturally and better run than their equivalents on the coast, which are more relaxed when responding to guests.

Rates are for a standard double room per night, including breakfast, but not including local taxes (usually 17 percent) and service charge (an extra 10 percent on the room rate plus tax).

Colombo

Casa Colombo
231 Galle Road, Colombo 4; tel: 011-452 0130; www.casacolombo.com; $$$$

Price for a double room for one night with breakfast:	
$$$$	over $200
$$$	$100–200
$$	$50–100
$	below $50

A recent addition to Colombo's chic hotels, this 200-year-old mansion has been lovingly restored and exquisitely decorated and after opening was touted as 'one of the hottest hotels in the world'. Each room is equipped with the latest high-tech gadgets, such as iPod docking stations. Watch out for the pink pool and glass sunbeds.

Cinnamon Grand
77 Galle Road, Colombo 3; tel: 011-243 7437; www.cinnamonhotels.com; $$$
One of the city's first five-star hotels when it was known as the Lanka Oberoi, this has been transformed after years of decline into the smartest place to stay if you want plenty of action, since it has nightly lobby entertainment, seven speciality restaurants and a British-style pub. Rooms are in two wings, with the swish executive-floor rooms in the original hotel block strung around an enormous atrium.

Cinnamon Lakeside
115 Sir Chittampalam A. Gardiner Mawatha, Colombo 2; tel: 011-249 1000; www.cinnamonhotels.com; $$$
Another five-star hotel that has gone through various incarnations (its last one being the Trans Asia), this now sparkles with a lively lobby, sushi bar, coffee shop and a Singaporean-style deck restaurant beside the Beira Lake, as well as super Thai and Chinese restaurants. Rooms are solidly furnished.

Galadari

64 Lotus Road, Colombo 1;
tel: 011-254 4544; http://galadari
hotel.lk; $$

On the edge of the high-security zone, this hotel has the best doormen in town, knowledgeable and always ready to help. Rooms on all floors are huge with two double beds, but furnishings are basic, making this a popular hotel with regulars who don't want fancy furnishings. It has a Lebanese restaurant as well as a Chinese one, and a cocktail bar with splendid views of the Presidential Secretariat and the ocean.

Galle Face

2 Galle Road, Colombo 3;
tel: 011-254 1010; www.galleface
hotel.com; $$

Famous old colonial landmark in a peerless position on the oceanfront at the southern end of Galle Face Green. The hotel has bags of atmosphere, although rooms in the old wing are a bit musty and old-fashioned; those in the newly restored Regency Wing combine modern comforts with colonial grace. There's also a beautiful new spa, and several appealing restaurants and bars.

Hilton

2 Sir Chittampalam A. Gardiner
Mawatha, Colombo 2; tel: 011-249
2492; www.hilton.com; $$$

The swankiest of Colombo's five-star properties, although the lobby lounge can be swamped with people holding meetings over coffee or just people-watching. With two grades of executive floors as well as standard rooms, the hotel has several restaurants, an English-style pub and a swimming pool complex reached by a bridge over the road.

Renuka

328 Galle Road, Colombo 3;
tel: 011-257 3598; www.renuka
hotel.com; $$

Functional and comfortable business-oriented hotel on the Galle Road, conveniently central and lower-priced than its Fort counterparts. On the seaside of the busy Galle Road traffic noise can be intrusive, but back rooms are quieter. Linked by a bridge over a side road to its twin, called the Renuka City Hotel, which has newer, brighter rooms.

Tintagel

65 Rosmead Place, Colombo 7;
tel: 011-460 2060; www.tintagel
colombo.com; $$$$

With 10 stylishly decorated suites, this recently opened boutique hotel is where to stay if you want to name-drop. Formerly the residence of three prime ministers, it has been transformed into a mansion of eclectic delights by Shanth Fernando, the genius behind the Gallery Café and the Paradise Road store. An interior courtyard swimming pool, veranda dining and a club-like library add even more panache.

Above from far left: one of Casa Colombo's luxurious rooms; sophisticated decor at the Tintagel; enjoying a sundowner at the Galle Face.

Around Colombo: Mount Lavinia

Mount Lavinia

100 Hotel Road, Mount Lavinia;
tel: 011-271 5221; www.mount
laviniahotel.com; $$$

One of Sri Lanka's most famous old
hotels, this sprawling white landmark
grew up around a 19th-century gover-
nor's love nest. Modern extensions have
all but swallowed up the original man-
sion, but the hotel retains enough
colonial touches to set it apart from the
run-of-the-mill west-coast resorts. It
has a superb private beach, a gorgeous
Ayurveda centre and top-class food.

Around Colombo: Negombo

The Beach

Ethulkala, Negombo; tel: 031-227
3500; www.jetwinghotels.com; $$$

Negombo's only five-star hotel, on a
busy strip of beach at the northern end
of the resort area, with superbly designed
(but low-ceilinged) rooms, elegantly
furnished with lots of dark wood, crisp
white sheets and glass-walled bathrooms, giving it a boutique feel. There's
also excellent food and a big pool.

Price for a double room for one night with breakfast:	
$$$$	over $200
$$$	$100–200
$$	$50–100
$	below $50

West Coast: Bentota

Hotel Susanthas

Nikethana Road, Pitaramba,
Bentota; tel: 034-227 5324;
www.hotelsusanthas.com; $

Bentota is a popular place to stay on
the island's west coast, and Hotel
Susanthas is a favourite budget option.
Access to the beach is by steps to the
adjoining railway platform and then
crossing over the single track. Rooms
are basic but clean, and open onto a
garden filled with tropical flowers.
There is an open-sided restaurant and
bar, but guests prefer to eat outside in
the garden, from a Western-oriented
à la carte menu (there's a pizza oven
too). Popular with long-stay guests
who like being able to please themselves, as well as with Sri Lankans.

Paradise Road The Villa Bentota

138/18 Galle Road, Bentota;
tel: 034-227 5311; www.villa
bentota.com; $$$$

Converted by designer/entrepreneur
Shanth Fernando from the late
architect Geoffrey Bawa's Mohotti
Villa, this has become the choicest
place to stay on the coast. There are
16 suites, stylishly furnished with
contemporary bathrooms and sea-
view verandas or large balconies, four
lounges and a 25m/yd swimming
pool, together with a Villa Café
along the lines of Fernando's Gallery
Café in Colombo.

West Coast: Ahungala

Heritance Ahungalla

Ahungalla; tel: 091-555 5000;
www.heritancehotels.com; $$$

One of the west coast's landmark resort hotels, with a 300m/yd drive from the main road through a coconut grove to the astonishing sight of the hotel entrance framing a view of its swimming pool and the Indian Ocean beyond. Spartan in decor and charm in spite of recent renovation, this five-star hotel lost cachet during Sri Lanka's downturn in tourism and is struggling to regain its upmarket image. Two restaurants and a coffee shop.

Kandy

Helga's Folly

32 Frederick E. Silva Mawatha,
Kandy; tel: 081-223 4571;
www.helgasfolly.com; $$$

Marvellously maverick hotel, set in a glorious position high above Kandy. The interior is like a kind of eccentric museum, filled with huge quantities of bric-a-brac ranging from animal heads and colonial photos to Indonesian puppets and huge candles covered in clumps of solidified wax. All rooms are individually decorated with colourful murals. The dispensary bar, cluttered nooks and crannies, laidback service, absence of package tourists, and occasional appearances by Madame Helga herself, are all part of the charm.

Queen's

4 Dalada Veediya, Kandy; tel: 081-574 5745; www.ceylonhotels.lk; $$

This venerable hotel is worth staying at for its location, right opposite the Temple of the Tooth, and for its nostalgic value, although its rooms are creaky. Now under the same management as the Galle Face Hotel and many of the country's rest houses, it has yet to be restored to its former grandeur.

Salika Inn

27/1 Rajapihilla Mawatha, Kandy; tel: 081-222 2365; www.salikainn.com; $

An amazing-value small guesthouse with breathtaking views of the Kandy Lake and Temple of the Tooth from its four bedrooms. Stylish but simple and a good base for exploring the region.

Hill Country: Gampola

Ellerton

Nuwa Gurukelle, Doluwa, Gampola; tel: 081-241 5137; www.ellerton srilanka.com; $$$

Owned by an English couple who, having bought the original bungalow and its abandoned mini-tea factory as a retirement residence, found so many people wanted to stay, they converted it into a hotel. There are three rooms in the main bungalow, and three more in the newly added Valley House; meals are taken in a separate dining pavilion, and there is a swimming pool with a view down a forested valley into the far distance.

Above from far left: sunset dining at The Beach; Helga's Folly has plenty of eccentric appeal.

Hill Country: Pussellawa

Lavender House

Hellbodde Estate, Katukitula, Pussellawa; tel: 052-225 9928; www.thelavenderhouseceylon.com; $$$$

With a wooden shingle roof, this restored plantation bungalow has five comfortable bedrooms, each one with French windows opening onto a private garden. The house is furnished with a touch of 1950s kitsch, including a portrait of Winston Churchill over the fireplace. A swimming pool overlooking tea gardens adds to the charm.

Hill Country: Nuwara Eliya

Glendower

5 Grand Hotel Road, Nuwara Eliya; tel: 052-222 2501; email: hotel_glendower@hotmail.com; $$

Small and extremely cosy faux-colonial bungalow hotel in a leafy setting by the golf course. Its nine rooms have polished wooden floors and furniture, and beds with plenty of blankets and quilts. The breakfast room transforms into the King Prawn Chinese restaurant for lunch and dinner, and there's a welcoming pub plus a roaring log fire in the lounge.

Price for a double room for one night with breakfast:	
$$$$	over $200
$$$	$100–200
$$	$50–100
$	below $50

Grand

Grand Hotel Road, Nuwara Eliya; tel: 052-222 2881; www.tangerinehotels.com; $$$

This lawn-fronted colonial hotel is one of Nuwara Eliya's major landmarks. Its imposing exterior and public areas, with long lounge and dining hall the size of a ballroom, as well as a snuggery bar and a billiard hall, are evocative of Edwardian days. The rooms are well worn, while those in the new Golf Wing are larger and brighter.

Heritance Tea Factory

Kandapola, Nuwara Eliya; tel: 052-222 9600; www.heritancehotels.com; $$$

One of Sri Lanka's most ingenious hotels, created by converting a tea factory – the exterior has been painstakingly preserved while the interior has been magically transformed into a cosy five-star hotel, with lots of old tea-making memorabilia on display. At the highest elevation (2,200m/ 7,214ft) of any hotel in Sri Lanka, its amazing setting, surrounded by tea plantations as far as the eye can see, is a major draw.

Hill Club

Grand Hotel Road, Nuwara Eliya; tel: 052-222 2653; www.hillclubsrilanka.net; $$$

Set in a 1930s mock-Gothic building close to the town centre, this famous colonial hotel offers a real taste of the

Ceylon of yesteryear. Mobile phones and children under 16 are banned, and the interior reeks of nostalgia, with a musty library, casual and residents' bars plus assorted stuffed stags' heads and cracked leather furniture. Accommodation is in neat, slightly chintzy rooms with creaking wood floors.

St Andrew's

10 St Andrew's Drive, Nuwara Eliya; tel: 052-222 3031; www.jetwing hotels.com; $$

At the opposite end of the town to the Grand Hotel and Hill Club, with a fine view overlooking the Golf Club, this is a colonial-period hotel with comfortable rooms steeped in nostalgia in the old wing, while those in the new wing have almost a ski-lodge ambience with pine as well as palm wood panelling. A walk-in wine cellar is a welcome addition to its sometimes draughty dining hall.

Ella Adventure Park

Uva Karandagolla; tel: 060-255 5038; www.wildernesslanka.com; $$

Accommodation is in cabanas, built among the trees and designed to blend perfectly with the surrounding forest. In keeping with the owners' passion for nature, the cabanas were constructed from granite, with none of the existing trees having to be cut down. They are secluded from each other by thick foliage, and some of

them are actually set in the trees. Furniture is made mostly from natural materials. Tents are also available for the adventurous.

Chaaya Village

Habarana; tel: 066-227 0047; www.chaayahotels.com; $$

This shares an entrance drive with its neighbour Cinnamon Lodge and is run by the same company, but there the similarity ends. It is sprawled across luxuriant land bordering a stunning lake, with rooms in village-style cabins, each recently and ingeniously refurbished, offering comfort and convenience. A triangular swimming pool with three levels that seems to taper off into the jungle is a recent addition. It is an informal, jolly place to stay, with all meals served as buffets, and with an open-sided bar, a jungle gym and a jogging track.

Cinnamon Lodge

Habarana; tel: 066-227 0011; www.cinnamonhotels.com; $$$

Set in a forested park around a lake, this resort's rooms are built as local-style villas with either a veranda or balcony and intriguing, Kandyan-style interiors with arches, alcoves and valances. Although there are 140 rooms, there is plenty of space, and they are linked by stone footpaths laid out along the lines of the nearby ancient Ritigala rock temple. Watch

Above from far left: the comfortable rooms at St Andrew's overlook the Golf Club; self-service dining at Chaaya Village.

out for inquisitive monkeys when walking in the grounds, and large squirrels begging for bread at breakfast. As well as dining in the main restaurant, meals can be taken by the lake or in the garden.

Cultural Triangle: Dambulla

Heritance Kandalama
Kandalama, Dambulla; tel: 066-555 5000; www.heritancehotels.com; $$$

Modern architecture cleverly blended into a cliff face makes this hotel a destination in itself for fans of minimalist design. The concrete lattice columns that front it are gradually being taken over by nature and have become jungle alleys for prowling monkeys who peer in the room windows at guests. Rooms are equipped with chunky wooden furniture while many of the fittings and walls are black, letting nature's greenery outside provide the colour. There are three swimming pools, if you can find them – the hotel stretches over a kilometre from one end to the other. One is by the reception tunnel and provides a soaring lake view. Meals are elaborate buffets.

Price for a double room for one night with breakfast:

$$$$	over $200
$$$	$100–200
$$	$50–100
$	below $50

East Coast: Trincomalee

Chaaya Blu
Sampaltivu Post, Uppuveli; tel: 026-222 2307; www.chaaya hotels.com; $$$

A trendy new name and a refurbished retro decor have been given to this old east-coast favourite, which was much loved in its former incarnation as Club Oceanic. The cottages at the edge of the broad beach remain, so guests can step from their patio straight onto the glorious stretch of sand disappearing into the distance at either side. There is a new swimming pool, and a fine presentation of buffet meals that include the hotel's famous spicy crab curry.

Welcombe Hotel
66 Lower Road, Orr's Hill, Trincomalee; tel: 026-222 3885; www.welcombehotel.com; $$

Built in the 1930s, this hotel has undergone several changes over the years – from Trincomalee's favourite hostelry to being taken over by the army in the 1990s. Modern additions of metal and concrete sit uncomfortably on its exterior, but glass panels and air-conditioning brighten its interior. The 1930s wood-panelled bar remains intact, however, as does the spirit of polite hospitality. Its position at the top of a very steep hill commands the finest views over Trincomalee's harbour. The restaurant offers seafood, oriental, European and Sri Lankan cuisines.

South Coast: Galle

Amangalla

10 Church Street, Fort; 091-239
2118; www.amanresorts.com; $$$$
Formerly the legendary New Oriental
Hotel, Galle's oldest, and now part of
the Aman chain, the Amangalla ranks
among the most expensive hotels in
Sri Lanka. Restoration has brightened
it and pitched it to appeal to the
sophisticated traveller who wants
everything to be just right and is prepared to pay for it. The precious
antique charm, however, seems a bit
artificial set against the laidback, unre-
constructed ambience of Galle Fort.

Galle Fort

28 Church Street, Fort; tel: 091-223
2870; www.galleforthotel.com; $$$
In 2005 an abandoned Dutch mansion
and warehouse was opened to guests
after being converted by an Australian
film producer and his Malaysian
banker partner as the Galle Fort
Hotel. Brightly original in decor, with
nine exotically furnished suites and
three rooms grouped around an inner
courtyard swimming pool, and notable
Asian-fusion style cuisine, the hotel
attracts the fun-loving cognoscenti.

Sun House

18 Upper Dickson Road, Galle;
tel: 091-438 0275; www.thesun
house.com; $$$$
An unexpected discovery up a road
leading inland from Galle town,
hidden behind a formidable gate, the
Sun House has been created from an
1860 mansion with suites stuffed with
designer knick-knacks and an ambi-
ence of assured gentility. Guests feel
they are at home here.

South Coast: Unawatuna

Unawatuna Beach Resort

Unawatuna; tel: 091-438 4545;
www.unawatunabeachresort.com; $$
Unawatuna's only real hotel, with 63
rooms in several styles ranging from
fisherman rustic to contemporary
splendour in the original beachfront
building and in its new annexe with
private pool. You can step out onto the
beach from its restaurant or bar
pavilion to swim or find all-night
party action. Ideal for those who want
organised accommodation rather than
the carefree ambience of Unawatuna's
many independent guesthouses.

South Coast: Yala

Yala Village

Kirinda, Tissamaharama; tel: 047-223
9450; www.johnkeellshotels.com; $$$
Over 50 chalets with jungle-themed
decor are set in a huge, unfenced area
at the borders of the Yala National
Park where wild animals roam. Cha-
lets have composition roof, particle
board ceilings and mock timber fur-
niture to complement the surrounding
wilderness without plundering it. Per-
fect tranquillity in a conserved natural
setting by beach and lake.

Above from far
left: the Heritance
chain combines
chic decor with
stunning locations.

All Sri Lankan hotels, even the smallest guesthouse, have a restaurant of some kind to cater for guests staying on a half-board package. Many also cater for non-residents, which is why, except in Colombo, there are very few independent restaurants.

Colombo's five-star hotels have 24-hour coffee shops where meals are self-service from a buffet, as well as speciality (like Chinese or Thai) and 'fine dining' (Western-style) restaurants. The city also has restaurants serving Sri Lankan, Italian, Indian, Korean, Chinese, Thai and Japanese cuisines.

The most convenient places for lunch while touring are country rest houses, where rice and curry is fresh and quickly served. Evening meals at other eateries out of Colombo will mostly be fried or grilled items from an à la carte menu.

Price guides are per person for two courses; local taxes of up to 17 percent and 10 percent service are extra.

Colombo

Banana Leaf

86 Galle Road, Colombo 3; tel: 011- 258 4403; daily 11am–3.30pm, 6–9.30pm; $

Price guide for a two-course meal for one:	
$$$$	over Rs2,500
$$$	Rs1,250–2,500
$$	Rs500–1,250
$	below Rs500

Cheap and cheerful first-floor café offering a range of Sri Lankan food, with set rice and curry and *biriyanis* served on banana-leaf plates. Regulars go for its delicious crab curry.

Bavarian

11 Galle Face Court 2, Colombo 3; tel: 011-242 1577; daily noon–3pm; 6–11pm; $$$

Opposite the Galle Face Hotel in an old residential and shopping terrace, this restaurant specialises in huge portions of German dishes, like roast pork knuckle with lots of sauces and an ample sausage platter. Satisfying comfort food if you are suffering from a surfeit of rice and curry. Tables are wooden slabs, seating is at wooden benches and, yes, there is draught (local) beer.

Bay Leaf

79 Gregory's Road, Colombo 7; tel: 011-269 5920; daily 11am–11pm; $$

The accent's on Italian food at this restaurant converted from an old colonial house in the diplomats' district of Colombo, and popular with expatriate residents. With lots of dining rooms, a veranda, and a bar in a bold, modern decor, it is a popular evening haunt, though lunch is also available. Pizzas are the hot favourite, sold under the brand name of the owner, Harpo, who also has outlets at the Odel shopping mall. More unusual dishes include soup served in a hollowed-out loaf of brown bread.

California Grill

Galadari Hotel, 64 Lotus Road,
Colombo 1; tel: 011-254 4544;
daily 7–11pm; $$$$

A reminder of days when the Galadari
Hotel was American-operated, the
California Grill retains its US style with
smartly dressed waiters offering a menu
of American and continental cuisine,
with steaks being a favourite, and Cali-
fornian wines by the glass. On the
rooftop floor of the hotel, the restaurant
has unbeatable views south to Galle
Face Green. With a pianist or trio providing music, this is the place for a
memorable evening.

Chesa Swiss

3 Deal Place A, Colombo 3;
tel: 011-257 3433; daily 7–11pm,
except public holidays; $$$$

One of the smartest restaurants in
Colombo, set in a charming colonial
villa and offering a sumptuously prepared range of Swiss food, Australian
steaks, seafood and vegetarian dishes.
It has a discreet cocktail bar and an
upmarket atmosphere.

Emperor's Wok

Colombo Hilton, 2 Sir Chittampalam
A. Gardiner Mawatha, Colombo 2;
tel: 011-254 4644; daily 12.30–3pm,
7.30–11pm; $$$

You have to walk through the hotel's
coffee shop (Spices) to find this res-
taurant for grand dining, Chinese-style,
with glittery decor and an excellent

choice of Sichuan cuisine, Peking
duck, special barbecue pork dishes and
dim sum. There is a special lunch
choice, but guests mostly go for the à
la carte menu with its attractively pre-
sented dishes. There is a show kitchen
at one end and a private dining room
available for groups.

Green Cabin

453 Galle Road, Colombo 3;
tel: 011-228 8011; daily 8am–8pm; $
Excellent little Sri Lankan café, long
established and patronised mainly by
locals, but an ideal place to test-drive
the local cuisine at low prices. The food
is based on the 'short eat' principle of
snacks ranging from bacon and egg pies
to *lamprais*, and hoppers and curry.

London Grill

Cinnamon Grand, 77 Galle Road,
Colombo 3; tel: 011-243 7437;
www.cinnamonhotels.com; daily
7–11pm $$$$

In the basement of the Cinnamon
Grand Hotel, this restaurant is the
genuine thing: an unreconstructed
1970s steakhouse, with original plush
decor and banquette seating. The
menu runs the full gamut of steaks,
grills, game and seafood, and the sen-
sational preparations are matched by
courteous and efficient service. The
place for a celebration dinner or just
to discover that it is possible to enjoy
traditionally prepared top-notch con-
tinental dishes in Sri Lanka.

Above from far
left: tasty *biryani*;
fresh chilli peppers;
Emperor's Wok.

Long Feng

Cinnamon Lakeside, 115 Sir
Chittampalam A. Gardiner Mawatha,
Colombo 2; tel: 011-249 1000;
www.cinnamonhotels.com; daily
noon–2.30pm, 7–11pm; $$$

In the centre of the hotel's corridor of restaurants, the Long Feng has been revamped in classic all-white decor and concentrating on Singaporean dishes. Choose between spicy dishes such as battered bean curd and pork belly or milder choices like sizzling lamb and leeks. The small portions will serve three people and the service is prompt.

Mango Tree

82 Dharmapala Mawatha, Colombo
3; tel: 011-587 9790; daily
noon–3pm, 7–11pm; $$$

Very popular upmarket North Indian restaurant, with a chic setting, reliable cuisine and excellent service. Because of its popularity with locals, advance reservation is advised.

Raja Bojun

Seylan Towers, 90 Galle Road,
Colombo 3; tel: 011-471 6171; daily
noon–4pm, 7pm–midnight, except
Poya days; $$

On the first floor of a bank building with a sweeping view of the Indian Ocean, this restaurant caters for the local palate with lunch and evening buffets of Sri Lankan curries and several kinds of rice at an amazingly low price. Dinner is also available from an

à la carte menu, but that seems superfluous as practically everything you could want is available on the buffet.

Royal Thai

Cinnamon Lakeside, 115 Sir
Chittampalam A. Gardiner Mawatha,
Colombo 2; tel: 011-249 1000;
www.cinnamonhotels.com; daily
noon–2.30pm, 7–11pm; $$$

This lavish Thai restaurant overlooks the hotel's garden, pool and lake, with exquisite decor matched by staff in traditional Thai costumes. The menu has an excellent selection of fiery dishes, including standards like green and red curries, pad thai and more unusual regional specialities. It is so popular that reservation is essential, even for lunch.

Spoons

Colombo Hilton, 2 Sir Chittampalam
A. Gardiner Mawatha, Colombo 2;
tel: 011-249 2492; Mon–Fri noon–
2.30pm, daily 7–11pm; $$$$

With glass-topped tables and an open kitchen where chefs perform, the decor of Spoons reflects its approach to food: contemporary and cutely presented,

Price guide for a two-course meal for one:	
$$$$	over Rs2,500
$$$	Rs1,250–2,500
$$	Rs500–1,250
$	below Rs500

with innovative variations on the traditional. Lunch is a selection of items from the table d'hôte menu, while dinner is a splendid à la carte affair with steaks, seafood and even caviar.

Thambapani

496/1 Duplication Road, Colombo 3; tel: 011-250 0615; Mon–Sat 11am–11pm; $$

Set in an old house, with tables inside or on the garden veranda, Thambapani specialises in island cuisine. This means items like Dutch *lamprais*, chilli crab and *biriyani*, but also includes mixed grills and pasta. There is a permanent exhibition of paintings by Sri Lankan artists for sale, which helps create the restaurant's charming and relaxed ambience.

1864

Galle Face Hotel, 2 Galle Road, Colombo 3; tel: 011-254 1010; www.gallefacehotel.com; Mon–Fri noon–3pm, daily 7–10.45pm; $$$$

With a genuine Victorian warehouse decor of red brick topped off with exposed utility pipes, this restaurant reflects the historical background of the hotel. There is a set lunch and an à la carte menu with hearty dishes such as venison shank. Staff with black aprons are suitably polite, in keeping with the restaurant's image of exclusivity. Down a spiral staircase there is a cellar wine bar with tapas-style snacks on demand.

Golden Grill

National Tourist Resort, Bentota; tel: 034-227 5455; daily 10am–10pm: $$

Another beach resort institution, the Golden Grill has been open for 30 years with a menu that has hardly changed, and is totally dependable. It appeals to guests tired of hotel food as well as to Sri Lankans wanting good-quality and low-priced dishes with taste and flavour. The mixed grill with beef, chicken, pork, sausage, bacon, egg, three different vegetables, French fries and salad is the island's best. Curries (from mild to hot) are always available, and other specialities are fresh fish including shark, and flaming dishes, whether steak or the pineapple surprise dessert.

Refresh

384 Galle Road, Hikkaduwa; tel: 091-227 7810; www.refreshrestaurant. com; daily noon–11.30pm; $$

A long restaurant stretching from the main road down to the beach, progressing from the front veranda past a refrigerated display cabinet of fresh seafood, to a restaurant with a live lobster aquarium (choose your own) and a beachside pavilion. With over 200 items on the menu, available at any time during the day, Refresh is a hit with tourists who come for the lobster, the cuttlefish or pork and steak dishes prepared with special sauces and served quickly.

Above from far left: Royal Thai; vegetarians should have no problem in Sri Lanka; Spoons.

CREDITS

Insight Step by Step Sri Lanka
Written by: Royston Ellis
Series Editor: Clare Peel
Editor: Tom Stainer
Cartography Editors: Zoë Goodwin and James Macdonald
Map Production: Stephen Ramsay
Original Cartography: Berndston GmbH
Picture Manager: Steven Lawrence
Art Editors: Richard Cooke and Ian Spick
Photography: All photography Sylvaine Poitau/APA except: Alamy 38-2, 60-1, 62-2; Vyacheslav Argenberg 59; Augapfel on Flickr 16-2, 38-4; AWL Images 40/41; Brian Bukowski 7-3; Casa Colombo 96-1; Chaaya Hotels & Resorts 101; Cinnamon Hotels 106-1; Corbis 2-5, 30; Fotolia 54-1, 104-1; Heritance Hotels 102/103 (all); Hilton Colombo 105, 107; Hafiz Issadeen 42; iStockphoto.com 8-7, 72-2, 81, 104-2; Jetwing Hotels 14-1, 23-1, 84-5/6, 98, 100-1/2; Jeroen Kurvers 38-3, 63; Bill Littman 44-3; James Manners 82-1; Towle Neu 82-2; onAsia 58-1; Noel Rodrigo/Leopard Safaris 83; Claire Rowland 97; Indi Samarajiva 8-4/5, 15-2, 17-1, 20, 21-1, 22-2, 26-4, 31, 34-1, 38-1, 39, 48-3/4, 60-2/3, 61-1, 80, 82-3, 92-1/2, 95; McKay Savage 6-5, 51-1; Scala Archives 24; Sri Lanka Tourism 2-2, 6-1, 15-1, 16-1; Still Pictures 28, 40-2; Chris Stowers/PANOS 32; Superstock 4-5, 37, 62-1; Tintagel 96-2; Nigel Wilson 99; Marcus Wilson Smith/APA 106-2.
Front cover: main image: photolibrary.com; bottom left and right: Sylvaine Poitau/APA
Printed by: CTPS-China

First Edition 2010

CONTACTING THE EDITORS

We would appreciate it if readers would alert us to errors or outdated information by writing to us at insight@apaguide.co.uk or APA Publications, PO Box 7910, London SE1 1WE, UK.

www.insightguides.com

DISTRIBUTION

Worldwide
APA Publications GmbH & Co. Verlag KG
(Singapore branch)
7030 Ang Mo Kio Ave 5
08-65 Northstar @ AMK
Singapore 569880
Tel: (65) 570 1051
E-mail: apasin@singnet.com.sg

UK and Ireland
GeoCenter International Ltd
Meridian House, Churchill Way West
Basingstoke, Hampshire, RG21 6YR
Tel: (44) 01256 817 987
E-mail: sales@geocenter.co.uk

United States
Langenscheidt Publishers, Inc.
36–36 33rd Street, 4th Floor
Long Island City, NY 11106
Tel: (1) 718 784 0055
E-mail: orders@langenscheidt.com

Australia
Universal Publishers
1 Waterloo Road, Macquarie Park, NSW 2113
Tel: (61) 2 9857 3700
E-mail: sales@universalpublishers.com.au

New Zealand
Hema Maps New Zealand Ltd (HNZ)
Unit 2, 10 Cryers Road
East Tamaki, Auckland 2013
Tel: (64) 9 273 6459
E-mail: sales.hema@clear.net.nz

INDEX